KU-215-534

Roger Scruton was professor of aesthetics at London's Birkbeck College 1985-92 and of philosophy at Boston University, Massachussetts 1992-94. He is now consulting editor of the *Salisbury Review*. His recent books include *Modern Philosophy* (1996), *Intelligent Person's Guide to Modern Culture* (1998), *Animal Rights or Wrongs* (2000) and *The Meaning of Conservatism* (2001).

What the critics said:

'This is a marvellous book which gives back to philosophy the sweep and depth it once had before linguistic analysis reduced it to a study of words and their meaning. Scruton is unafraid to take on big topics – God, truth, morality and freedom – with imagination and verve.'

Jonathan Sacks, *Financial Times*

'Scruton is brilliant at explaining how philosophical questions differ from scientific questions, how they are wider and more searching. The old question "how do we know that our beliefs are true?" is as worth asking of a modern materialist as of an old-fashioned Christian.'

A N Wilson, *Evening Standard*

'Scruton's forthrightness is exemplary: it teaches, implicitly, how to express disputes as well as seeking to resolve them.'

Frederic Raphael, *The Sunday Times*

'Scruton's method is to pursue his fox over a landscape of high fences – truth, doubt, personhood, time, deity, freedom, morality, sex, music and history – not just to run it down, but to have the exhilaration of the gallop. The result is stimulating and instructive.'

A C Grayling, *Times Literary Supplement*

'The *Guide* deserves to become a popular classic of non-technical philosophy. The chief merit of the *Guide* is that it shows how philosophical thinking can make a difference, not primarily by leading us to act upon the world but by changing our ways of thinking about it.'

John Haldane, *The Tablet*

'Scruton has considerable talent in condensing the complex arguments and ideas of the masters.

Philosophy isn't the only way of learning to think, but it is one of the best, and philosophy has no better salesman than Scruton.'

Tibor Fischer, *The Times*

'Here philosophers and their philosophies are signposts, rather than stopping points, on a philosophical pilgrimage which … traverses Descartes-type doubt, Fichte's solipism, God's death and post-modern relativism, to present a stoically optimistic hymn to humanity's transcendence.'

Jane O'Grady, *Times Educational Supplement*

'A compass for personal adventures into philosophy'

The Times, metro section (4/4/98)

'A lucid and accessible introduction to some of the central problems of this notoriously difficult subject.'

Robert L Pollock, *Wall Street Journal*

AN INTELLIGENT PERSON'S GUIDE
TO PHILOSOPHY

AN INTELLIGENT PERSON'S GUIDE TO PHILOSOPHY

Roger Scruton

Duckbacks

Published in 2002 by Duckbacks, a paperback imprint
of Duckworth Media Group

First published in 1996 by
Gerald Duckworth & Co. Ltd.
61 Frith Street, London W1D 3JL
Tel: 020 7434 4242
Fax: 020 7434 4420
Email: enquiries@duckworth-publishers.co.uk
www.ducknet.co.uk

© 1996 by Roger Scruton

All rights reserved. No part of this publication
may be reproduced, stored in a retrieval system, or
transmitted, in any form or by any means, electronic,
mechanical, photocopying, recording or otherwise,
without the prior permission of the publisher.

A catalogue record for this book is available
from the British Library

ISBN 0 7156 3206 X

Printed in Great Britain by
BOOKMARQUE Ltd, Croydon, Surrey

Contents

Preface

This book tries to make philosophy interesting; I have therefore focused on ideas which make philosophy interesting to *me*. From the academic point of view the result is far from orthodox; but my hope is that the reader will leave this book with a sense of philosophy's relevance, not just to intellectual questions, but to life in the modern world.

I refer here and there to the great philosophers, and in particular to Kant and Wittgenstein, who have been the most important influences on my thinking. But I make no attempt to give either a history or a survey of the subject. This book offers itself as a guide to the reader who is prepared to venture into philosophy, and presupposes no knowledge other than that which an intelligent person is likely to possess already.

Such a person will want to know, nevertheless, how the book relates to other productions in the field, and whether it belongs to a school of thought that is larger than itself – to some 'ology' or 'ism' which would serve to file it away in the ever-growing archive of the great unread. Suffice it to say that I came to philosophy as an undergraduate, being dissatisfied with a scientific education, and suspecting that there might be deep and serious questions to which science has no answer. But I encountered, in the academic subject of philosophy, reams of pseudo-science against which my conscience rebelled. Consequently I set out in search of a *literary* philosophy – not an ism but a prism, through which intellectual light would shine in many colours.

Philosophy is not the only subject that has been 'scientized' by the modern university: literature has been shrunk to 'literary theory', music has been colonized by set theory, Schenkerian analysis, and generative linguistics, and architecture has been all but abolished by engineering. Pretended science has driven honest speculation from the intellectual economy, just as bad money drives out good. This Gresham's law of the intellect operates wherever university teachers in the humanities exchange knowledge and imagination for the chimera of scientific 'research'. A philosopher should certainly make room for scholarship: but scholarship has no 'results', no explanatory 'theories', no methods of experimentation. It is, at best, a spiritual discipline, and what will emerge from scholarship depends intimately on the soul of the person who engages in it. When academic philosophers disguise their writings as scientific reports, and cultivate the fiction of step by step advances to a theory, we can be sure that something has gone wrong with their conception of the subject. The result is tedious to the student, partly because it is born of tedium – the tedium that comes when our world is surrendered to science. If this book has a message, it is that scientific truth has human illusion as its regular by-product, and that philosophy is our surest weapon in the attempt to rescue truth from this predicament.

We should not expect philosophy to be easy; nor can it be free from technicalities. For philosophical questions arise at the periphery of ordinary thinking, when words fail, and we address the unknown with an invented discourse. For this very reason the reader of philosophy must beware of frauds, who exploit the known difficulty of the subject in order to disguise unexamined premises as hard-won conclusions. One such fraud – Michel Foucault – features in what follows;

but my intention is not to create a *sottiserie* for our times, however much this might be needed. It is to mount a philosophical argument, which will show philosophy to be a natural extension of our interest in truth, and a therapy for our modern confusions.

I am grateful to Robin Baird-Smith, who encouraged me to write this book, and to David Wiggins, whose painstaking attempt to dissuade me from errors of logic and style absolves him from all responsibility for the many that remain. I am also grateful to Fiona Ellis and Sophie Jeffreys, the two intelligent women upon whom the book was first tried out, and who suggested vital improvements.

Malmesbury, Spring 1996

1

Why?

Philosophy – the 'love of wisdom' – can be approached in two ways: by doing it, or by studying how it has been done. The second way is familiar to university students, who find themselves confronted by the largest body of literature that has ever been devoted to a single subject. This book follows a more ancient pattern. It attempts to teach philosophy by doing it. Although I refer to the great philosophers, I give no reliable guide to their ideas. To expound their arguments in full dress would be to frustrate my chief purpose, which is to bring philosophy to life.

Life as we know it is not much like the life from which our philosophical tradition arose. Plato and Socrates were citizens of a small and intimate city state, with publicly accepted standards of virtue and taste, in which the educated class derived its outlook from a single collection of incomparable poetry, but in which all other forms of knowledge were rare and precious. The intellectual realm had not yet been divided into sovereign territories, and thought was an adventure which ranged freely in all directions, pausing in wonder before those chasms of the mind which we now know as philosophy. Unlike the great Athenians, we live in a crowded world of strangers, from which standards of taste have all but disappeared, in which the educated class retains no common culture, and in which knowledge has been parcelled out into specialisms, each asserting its monopoly interest against the waves of migrant ideas. Nothing in this world is fixed: intellectual life is one vast commotion, in which a myriad voices strive to be heard above the din. But as the quantity of communication increases, so does its quality decline; and the most important sign of this is that it is no longer acceptable to say so. To criticize popular taste is to invite the charge of élitism, and to defend distinctions of value – between the virtuous and the vicious, the beautiful and the ugly, the sacred and the profane, the true and the false – is to offend against the only value-judgement that is widely accepted, the judgement that judgements are wrong. In such circumstances the task of philosophy must change. Philosophy, for Plato, undermined the certainties of a common culture, and led, through doubt and wonder, to a realm of truth. Now there are no certainties, and no common culture worth the name. Doubt is the refrain of popular communication, scepticism extends in all directions, and philosophy has been deprived of its traditional starting point in the faith of a stable community. A philosophy that begins in doubt assails what no-one believes, and invites us to nothing believable. However important its achievement, in describing the nature and limits of rational thinking, such a philosophy now runs the risk of being disengaged from the life surrounding it, and of forswearing the ancient promise of philosophy, which is to help us, however indirectly, to live wisely and well.

In his justly celebrated book, *The Problems of Philosophy*, Bertrand Russell described philosophy in the terms implied in his title: as a series of problems. 'Philosophy is to be studied,' he wrote, 'not for the sake of any definite answers to its questions, since no definite answers can, as a rule, be known to be true, but rather for the sake of the questions themselves.' But what, we might ask, is the point of such a study? Why should we, who have so few answers, devote our energies to questions which have none? For Russell, the purpose is to become a 'free intellect, an intellect that will see as God might see, without a *here* and *now*, without hopes and fears, without the trammels of customary beliefs and traditional prejudices, calmly, dispassionately, in the sole and exclusive desire of knowledge – knowledge as impersonal, as purely contemplative, as it is possible for man to attain'. It is easy to be tempted by this vision of a purely abstract study, which is at the same time an exercise of the highest freedom, and a liberation from custom, prejudice and the here and now. But the mask of rhetoric is thin, and Russell's anxiety shines through it. He knows that we must live in the here and now, and that the difficulty of doing so arises precisely because the 'customary beliefs and traditional prejudices' have lost their credibility. We are hoping, fearing creatures, and without our hopes and fears we should be loveless and unlovable. To see calmly and dispassionately is right – but only sometimes, and only in respect of some subjects. Besides, Russell published those words in 1912, when scepticism was the luxury of a ruling class, and not the daily diet of humanity.

In emphasizing abstract questions, Russell is true to the history of philosophy. The virtue of such questions is in freeing us from self-interested illusions; they set us at a distance from the world of emotion, and enable us to see it for a moment as though we ourselves were not involved. But philosophers, like other human beings, have a tendency to represent their own way of life as the best way – perhaps as the sole way to redemption. Freeing themselves from one set of illusions, they fall prey to others, every bit as self-interested, and with the added advantage of ennobling the person who promotes them. They extol the 'dispassionate' and 'contemplative' life, since it is the life that they have chosen. They tell us, like Plato, that this life leads to a vision of a higher world, or like Spinoza, that it shows our world in another light, 'under the aspect of eternity'. They reproach us for our sensuous ways, and gently remind us, in the words of Socrates, that 'the unexamined life is not a life for a human being'. It is tempting to agree with Nietzsche, that the philosopher is not interested in truth, but only in *my* truth, and that the thing which masquerades as truth for him, is no more than the residue of his own emotions.

The judgement is not fair: none of Nietzsche's are. But it has a point. Philosophy in our tradition has assumed the existence of a plain, common-sense approach to things, which is the property of ordinary people, and which it is the business of philosophy to question. The result might be to subvert the normal view, as in Nietzsche himself; or it might be to question the question, as in Wittgenstein, and return us to our shared 'form of life' as the only thing we have. Nevertheless, without the background assumption, there is no normality to subvert or reaffirm, and philosophy finds it hard to begin. The peculiarity of our condition is that the assumption can no longer be made. Faced with the ruin of folkways, traditions, conventions, customs and dogmas, we can only feel a helpless tenderness for these things which have proved, like everything human, so much easier to destroy than to create. But what has philosophy to say in the face of this momentous change – the change, as some have described it, from modern scepticism, to the postmodern condition, in which all beliefs are simultaneously both doubted and affirmed, though in inverted commas?

The Czech philosopher T.G. Masaryk (1850-1937) ascribed many of the ills of the modern world to 'half-education'. It was the prominence in public life of the semi-educated, he suggested, that stirred up the hopes and destroyed the certainties of mankind. All faith was cast in doubt, all morality relativized, and all simple contentment destroyed, by the sarcastic criticism of those who could see just so far as to question the foundations of social order, but not so far as to uphold them.

Masaryk's complaint, like Russell's declaration of faith in abstract thought, belongs to another world – a world that was shortly to disappear in the turmoil of the Great War, from which Masaryk emerged as President of the newly formed state of Czechoslovakia. Nevertheless, it has a deep relevance for us, whose world has been rotted by scepticism, and who wish to know how to proceed, when no one offers guidance save those who are mocked for doing so. If half-education undermines our certainties, is there a whole education that restores them? Or does nothing remain at the end of all our thinking, save a handful of dust?

In this book I try to show what philosophy has to offer in this new condition. Its task, as I envisage it, is thoughtfully to restore what has been thoughtlessly damaged. This damaged thing is not religion, morality or culture, but the ordinary human world: the world in its innocence, the world in spite of science. Russell is surely right in his assumption that philosophy begins from questions; he is right too that it seeks for answers in a realm of abstraction, where ordinary interests recede, and contemplation comes in place of them. But its task does not end in this endless seeking. There is a way back to the human world, through the very abstract thinking which corrodes it.

We are rational beings, and it is in our nature to ask questions. Dogs and cats live in 'a world of perception', to use Schopenhauer's phrase. For them the present experience is everything, and thought no more than a fragile bridge of anticipation, which leads from this experience to the next one. We, however, are beset by the need to explain. Faced with something unusual, our thought is not 'What next?' but 'Why?' By answering the second of those questions, we can answer the first. And this, in brief, is the scientific method. So where does the difference lie, between science and philosophy? Or is philosophy just a kind of generalised science, as it was for its first practitioners – those Titanic figures like Thales and Heraclitus, who emerge from the prehistoric darkness to tell us that 'All is water,' or 'There is only fire,' and whose enigmatic words resound down the centuries like mysterious primeval cries? This question is of the first importance, since nothing has changed the position of philosophy so much as the success of modern science.

Scientific explanations give the causes of what we observe. But scientific knowledge would be far less useful than it is – no more useful than historical knowledge – if it could not be translated into predictions. The device whereby diagnosis becomes prediction is the 'causal law', the law which tells us not just that one event is the effect of another, but that events of the second kind make events of the first kind more likely. Feeling ill after drinking water from Alfred's tap, I may suspect that the water caused my illness. As yet this is only a hypothesis; it is confirmed when I discover that other people too, drinking from that tap, have contracted a similar illness. I venture the law that drinking from Alfred's tap makes illness likely. This statement is interesting for two reasons: first, it is open-ended: it does not refer only to cases so far observed, but universally. It has established its power as a diagnosis by becoming a prediction. Secondly, it is phrased in terms of probability: it does not say that everyone who drinks from Alfred's tap will become ill, but only that such an effect is likely. Likelihood, or probability, is measurable. If 60 per cent of observed cases have produced the given result, then we conclude that, on the evidence, there is a 60 per cent probability of the next case doing so as well.

That is a very rough piece of science. To the question 'Why was I ill?' it offers the answer 'Because I drank from Alfred's tap.' But this answer invites a further question: 'Why does drinking from Alfred's tap cause illness?' Such questions are pursued to the point where causal laws become 'laws of nature' – laws which do not merely record our observations, but which describe the underlying mechanism. We discover that an organism lives in Alfred's water tank, and that this organism can live also in the human digestive system, causing inflammation. It is a law of nature that organisms of this kind live in this way, and a law of nature that the human digestive system reacts as it does to their presence. This is not a statement of what we observe merely, but a statement of how things are. We can go deeper into the matter, discovering the precise chemical reaction which precipitates the inflammation, and so on. And the deeper we go, the firmer handle we acquire on the disease, the more likely we are to find a cure for it, and the more able are we to prevent it from spreading.

The nature and limits of scientific method are hotly debated among academic philosophers. But this much, at least, is suggested by my example. First, that the search for causes involves a search for laws; secondly, that laws are statements of probability; thirdly, that laws are themselves explained through wider and more general laws; fourthly, that however far we investigate the causes of something, we can always go further; and finally, that the further we go, the more remote we find ourselves from the world of observation. At the end of our enquiry we may be describing processes which are not observable at all – even processes, like those of quantum mechanics, which we could not observe, and which we can hardly describe in the language of observation. As quantum mechanics shows, the concept of probability, which features in our very first hypothesis, reappears in the final diagnosis: the world of nature is governed by laws, but no scientific law, however deep, is more than a statement of probability. Of nothing in the natural world can it be said that it *must* be so, but at best that it is highly likely to be so.

At a certain stage in its recent history, philosophy was dominated by the 'logical positivists', whose school originated in Vienna between the wars and whose ideas were brought to the English-reading public by A.J. Ayer, in his famous book, *Language, Truth and Logic* (1936). The positivists were fascinated by science, the results and methods of which seemed so clear and indisputable when set beside the pompous nonsense of philosophy. They sought to explain why people can argue fruitfully over scientific questions, from a common understanding of their meaning; whereas philosophical dispute seems endless, with each participant inventing the rules. They concluded that the mass of philosophical propositions are meaningless, and proposed, by way of clinching the matter, a criterion of meaning, called the 'verification principle'. This says that the meaning of a sentence is given by the method of its verification – by the procedure for determining whether it is true or false. Scientific propositions are meaningful, since they are tested by observation. No observation, experiment or analysis can settle whether 'The Absolute is One and All-embracing' is true; we should therefore dismiss the sentence as meaningless.

Logical positivism no longer has a following, and it is easy to see why. The verification principle cannot be verified: it therefore condemns itself as meaningless. Still, the positivists' view of science remains highly influential. Many philosophers regard observation not merely as the route to scientific truth but also as the true subject-matter of science. Laws and theories generalize from observations, and weave them into a seamless tapestry. In the last analysis, that is what they mean. Reality is systematic appearance, and theories are summaries of observations.

Look back at my example, and you will see how strange that picture is. Science may start from observation. Its purpose, however, is not to summarize appearance, but to distinguish appearance from reality. Science is a voyage of discovery, which passes from the observed to the unobserved, and thence to the unobservable. Its concepts and theories describe a reality so remote from the world of appearance that we can hardly envisage it, and while its findings are *tested* through observation, this is no more than a trivial consequence of the fact that observation is what 'testing' means. Science explains the appearance of the world, but does not describe it.

This means that the claim so often made on behalf of philosophy, that it shows the *reality* behind *appearances*, could equally, and more plausibly, be made on behalf of science. And if the methods of science are agreed, certain, and indisputable, while those of philosophy obscure, controversial and vague, what need have we of philosophy? What is the contribution that philosophy could make, to our vision of the world?

Here is one response to those questions. Science begins when we ask the question 'Why?' It leads us from the observed event to the laws which govern it, and onwards to higher and more general laws. But where does the process end? If each new answer prompts another question, then scientific explanations are either incomplete or endless (which is another way of being incomplete). But in that case science leaves at least one question unanswered. We still don't know why the series of causes exists: the why of this event may be found in that; but what of the why of the world? Cosmologists dispute over the 'origins of the universe', some arguing for a Big Bang, others for a slow condensation. But in the nature of the case, such theories leave a crucial question unanswered. Even if we conclude that the universe began at a certain time from nothing, there is something else that needs to be explained, namely, the 'initial conditions' which then obtained. Something was true of the universe at time zero, namely, that *this* great event was about to erupt into being, and to generate effects in accordance with laws that were already, at this initial instant, sovereign. And what is the why of *that*?

A positivist would dismiss such a question as meaningless. So too would many scientists. But if the only grounds for doing so is that science cannot answer it, then the response is self-serving. *Of course* the question has no scientific answer: it is the question beyond science, the question left over when all of science has been written down. It is a philosophical question.

Well yes, the sceptic will say; but it does not follow that it has an answer. Maybe philosophical questions arise at the margin of our thinking, where the writ of reason ceases to run, and no more answers are forthcoming. Kant, in the *Critique of Pure Reason*, tried to show that this might be so. But it required a philosopher to argue the point, and if Kant is right, then at least one philosophical question has an answer. For it is a philosophical and not a scientific question, whether the question as to the explanation of the universe has an answer; and the answer, according to Kant, is no.

Not all philosophers have agreed with him. There is an argument, known by the name bestowed on it by Kant, but due to St Anselm, eleventh-century archbishop of Canterbury, which offers the complete and final explanation of everything, by showing that at least one thing exists *of necessity*. The 'ontological argument' is normally offered as a proof of the existence of God. But it is capable of a wider interpretation, and reappears in Spinoza and Hegel as the final answer to every 'Why?' It tells us that God is, by definition, the sum of all perfections, so that existence, which is part of perfection, belongs to his essence. He *must* exist, and the question why he exists answers *itself*. Since God's existence explains everything else, no 'Why?' is without an answer, not even the why of the world.

Stated thus briefly and bluntly, the argument has the appearance of a sophism. Hence it is never stated briefly or bluntly, but wrapped in artful subtleties. Indeed, it is the one argument for God's existence that is still alive, and which perhaps always *was* alive, even before St Anselm gave explicit voice to it. For what is really meant by the sublime words which open the Gospel according to St John? In the beginning, writes the evangelist, was the word, the *logos*. In Greek philosophy *logos* means not only word, but reason, argument, account: any answer to the question 'Why?' In other words, or rather, in the same words if you stick to the Greek: In the beginning was the why which answers itself.

Goethe's Faust, meditating on this passage, offers an improvement: not words but deeds begin things, and if the world has sense for us, it is because *im Anfang war die Tat*: in the beginning was the deed. Let us not ask 'Whose deed?', for such a question merely plunges us again into the endless stream of causes. Let us ask instead how the 'Why?' of things is changed, when we see them not merely as events but as actions. When the judge asks me why I put arsenic in my wife's tea, he will not be satisfied by my saying 'Because electrical impulses from my brain caused my hand to reach for the bottle and tip it into the waiting teacup' – although that may be a true answer to the question 'Why?' construed as scientists construe it, as a request for the cause. For it is an answer *of the wrong kind*.

It seems, then, that the question 'Why?' is ambiguous. Sometimes it is answered by pointing to a cause, sometimes by pointing to a *reason*. The judge is asking what I was *aiming* at. If I reply that I had mistaken the bottle for that which contained the whisky, that I had intended to administer only a small dose of arsenic as a warning shot, or that I had intended to kill her since quite frankly enough was enough – then I have in each case offered a reason for my action, and the reply is pertinent. There are philosophers who say that reasons are causes, though causes of a special kind. For the three replies that I have sketched are valid explanations, and what is an explanation, if it does not mention a cause? But this does not get to the heart of the matter. The peculiarity of reasons is that you can argue with them; you can accept them or reject them; you can offer counter-reasons, and praise or condemn the agent on account of them. Even if reasons are causes, they have been lifted from the neutral realm of scientific theory, and endowed with a moral sense.

The ambiguity here can be phrased in another way. Sometimes we explain our actions; sometimes we justify them. And while explanations are either true or false, reasons can be good or bad. They belong to the endless moral dialogue whereby people relate to one another and to the world, and it is not surprising if they have an entirely different structure, and make use of entirely different concepts, from the explanations offered by the science of behaviour. My original answer to the judge was absurd not because it was false, but because it removed my action from the sphere of judgement, and described it in terms that make no reference to it as *mine*. Yet these are precisely the terms that we should expect the science of behaviour to employ: for they identify the *underlying mechanism* that explains what we observe.

We encounter here, and not for the first time in this work, an enduring paradox. It seems that we describe the world in two quite different ways – as the world which *contains* us, and as the world on which we act. We are part of nature, obedient to natural laws. But we also stand back from nature, and make choices which we believe to be free. Nature has a meaning for us – many meanings – and we classify it in ways which could find no place in scientific theory. When we see another's smile we see human flesh moving in obedience to impulses in the nerves. No law of nature is suspended in this process; we smile not in spite of, but because of, nature. Nevertheless, we understand a smile in quite another way: not as flesh, but as spirit, freely revealed. A smile is always more than flesh for us, even if it is only flesh.

The question 'Why?', when asked of a smile, is seeking a meaning. Perhaps you are smiling for a reason; but even if you have no reason, there may be a why to your smile. I may understand it as a gesture of serene acceptance. And that answers the question why you smile, even though it names neither justification nor cause. The description *makes the smile intelligible*. So here is another 'Why?', and one that can be applied more widely than to human beings. The why of a note in music, or a line in a painting, is like this. We understand why the opening chord of *Tristan* resolves onto the dominant seventh of A minor, not by learning Wagner's reason for writing this, still less by looking for a cause, but by grasping the weight of these two chords as they balance against each other, by hearing the voice-leading which moves between them, and by pausing with the music, in the expectation of another resolution that never comes. Criticism describes the why of this music; but you do not need the description in order to understand what you hear, any more than you need a description to understand a smile. Understanding is *sui generis*, part of our way of relating to the world, when we relate to it as free beings.

And here we encounter another task for philosophy, and perhaps its most important task in our conditions. When we respond to the world as free beings, we look for meanings and reasons, and divide the world according to our interests, and not according to its inner nature, as this is revealed to science. Indeed, the meaning of the world is enshrined in conceptions which, while indispensable to the 'Why?' of freedom, find no place in the language of science: conceptions like beauty, goodness and spirit which grow in the thin topsoil of human discourse. This topsoil is quickly eroded when the flora are cleared from it, and there is a risk that nothing will ever grow thereafter. You can see the process at work in the matter of sex. Human sexuality has usually been understood through ideas of love and belonging. An enchanted grove of literary ideas and images protected those conceptions, and man and woman lived within it happily, or at any rate, with a manageable unhappiness. The sexologist clears all this tangled undergrowth away, to reveal the scientific truth of things: the animal organs, the unmoralized impulses, and the tingling sensations that figure in those grim reports on the behaviour of American humanoids. The *meaning* of the experience plays no part in the scientific description. Since science has, or at any rate assumes, absolute sovereignty over what is true, the meaning comes to be viewed as a fiction. People may briefly try to reinvent it, sometimes even hoping to do a better job. Failing, however, they lapse into a state of cynical hedonism, scoffing at the fogeys who believe there is more to sex than biology.

That is an example of a process which the great sociologist Max Weber (1864-1920) called *Entzauberung* – disenchantment. Philosophy is useful to us, precisely because it, and it alone, can vindicate the concepts through which we understand and act on the world: concepts like that of the person, which have no place in science but which describe what we understand, when we relate to the world as it truly is for us. The scientific attempt to explore the 'depth' of human things is accompanied by a singular danger. For it threatens to destroy our response to the surface. Yet it is on the surface that we live and act: it is there that we are created, as complex appearances sustained by the social interaction which we, as appearances, also create. It is in this thin topsoil that the seeds of human happiness are sown, and the reckless desire to scrape it away – a desire which has inspired all those 'sciences of man', from Marx and Freud to sociobiology – deprives us of our consolation. Philosophy is important, therefore, as an exercise in conceptual ecology. It is a last-ditch attempt to re-enchant the world, and thereby 'save the appearances'. And as Oscar Wilde said, it is only a very shallow person who does not judge by appearances.

Philosophy arises, therefore, in two contrasted ways: first, in attempting to complete the 'Why?' of explanation; secondly in attempting to justify the other kinds of 'Why?' – the 'Why?' which looks for a reason, and the 'Why?' which looks for a meaning. Most of the traditional branches of the subject stem from these two attempts, the first of which is hopeless, the second of which is our best source of hope.

2

Truth

Most, but not all. For there is another and vital task for philosophy, which is pertinent in all times and places, and no less urgent for us than it was for Plato. This is the task of criticism. In seeking ultimate explanations, and durable meanings, philosophy is engaged in constructive tasks. It is explaining the world, and telling us how to live in it. But philosophy also has a negative task, which is to analyse and criticize human thinking, to ask awkward questions like 'How do you know?' and 'What do you mean?' Two branches of the subject – epistemology (the theory of knowledge) and logic – have grown in answer to these questions, and they will guide us through the next two brief, but necessary, chapters.

There are no truths, said Nietzsche, only interpretations. Logic cries out against this remark. For is it true? Well, only if there are no truths. In other words, only if it is not true. Nietzsche is widely revered for his 'iconoclastic' epistemology, and cited as an authority by modernists, structuralists, postmodernists, poststructuralists, postpostmodernists ... indeed, just about anyone who has no patience with the idea of authority. Certainly, Nietzsche was a genius, a great writer, and one of the few who have peered into the abyss and recorded, in the brief moment of sanity that then remains, just how it looks. We should be grateful to him, since real warnings are rare. But we should also be warned. Don't come down this path, his writings tell us, for this way madness lies.

All discourse and dialogue depend upon the concept of truth. To agree with another is to accept the truth of what he says; to disagree is to reject it. In ordinary speech we aim at truth, and it is only on the assumption of this aim that people make sense. Imagine trying to learn French in a society of monolingual Frenchmen, without making the assumption that, in general, they aim to speak truly. Of course, not everything we say is true: sometimes we make mistakes, sometimes we tell lies or half-truths. But without the concept of truth, and its sovereign standing in our discourse, we could not tell lies; nor could we have the concept of a mistake.

Truth is sovereign too in rational argument. From the beginning of history people have needed to distinguish valid from invalid arguments, and no word in the language is more smooth from the touch of human need than 'if' – the sign that discourse has shifted from statement to hypothesis, and that a deduction has begun. 'If p then q; not-q therefore not-p.' Such is our paradigm of valid inference, and only a lunatic would reject it. But what do we mean by 'valid'? Surely, an argument is valid when it is impossible that the premises should be true, and the conclusion false. Validity is defined in terms of truth.

It is an odd fact that logic, which ought to be the most scientific part of philosophy, is in many ways the most controversial, and also the slowest to change. Aristotle summarized and classified the valid 'syllogisms', and gave a subtle account of truth and inference. But nobody built on his achievement until modern times. Although Leibniz made some important advances, the knowledge of logic among philosophers actually *declined* during the nineteenth century. The greatest nineteenth-century philosopher – Hegel – wrote a book called *Logic* which contains only invalid arguments. It was not until the work of two philosophical mathematicians, George Boole (1815-1864) and Gottlob Frege (1848-1925), that the subject began to make progress. And it is testimony to the scientific nature of logic that there was progress to be made. (You don't make *progress* in art, literature or religion.)

The structure of language and rational argument can be understood, according to Frege, only if we make a distinction between the sense of our words, and their reference. 'The Morning Star' has a different sense from 'The Evening Star', but it refers to the same thing. The sense of a phrase is what we understand when we understand it. The reference is the object or concept 'picked out' – in this case the planet Venus, the star which appears first in the morning and last at night. The distinction between sense and reference runs through all language. Names and descriptions, predicates and relational terms, prepositions and connectives – all have both sense and reference, as do sentences themselves. We can apply the distinction to sentences, Frege argued, by recognizing the deep relation between language and truth. If we assign to each sentence a 'truth-value', according to whether it is true or false, then we find that, from the point of view of logic, the truth-value stands to the sentence as the object stands to its name. We understand a sentence when we know the difference that would be made to the world, were the sentence to be true: in other words, the sense of a sentence is given by the conditions for its truth. Truth-value, and truth-conditions, give the two dimensions of sentence-meaning.

The emphasis on truth provides a clue to the structure of language. When we join two sentences with the word 'and', we form a new sentence which is true when its component parts are both true, otherwise false. That is how we grasp the word 'and'. It refers to an operation defined in terms of truth-values. The same goes for other words which form new

sentences from old ones – including 'if', 'not', and 'or'. Seeing
language in this way, we begin to make sense of its structure. We see how it is that, from a finite array of words,
infinitely many sentences can be constructed and understood. We begin to distinguish the valid from the invalid
arguments, the well-formed from the ill-formed complexes,
and the different functions of the parts of speech. For example, we can begin to describe the real logical difference
between names, which refer to objects, predicates, which
refer to concepts, and 'quantifiers' like 'some' and 'all', which
have a logical role of their own.

Modern logic emphasizes the distinction between syntax
and semantics. Language is built from a finite vocabulary,
according to 'syntactic rules' which tell us which strings of
words are acceptable and which are deviant. But these rules
are incomplete without the rules of semantics. Semantic
rules assign 'values' to the terms of a language: in other
words, they assign an object to each name, a concept (or
class) to each predicate, a function to each connective, and
so on. And they show how to evaluate a complete sentence
in terms of the values of its parts. Semantic rules can be
constructed only in the way sketched by Frege: by assuming
that sentences are assessed in terms of their truth-value.
Without this assumption syntax is arbitrary, assertion
pointless, and rational discourse impossible to explain.
Since philosophy begins from rational discourse – and in
particular, from the question 'Why?' – philosophy is commit-
ted to at least one, all-important claim: namely, that there
is a real distinction between the true and the false.

'*What is truth?* said jesting Pilate, and would not stay for
an answer.' The famous words which begin Bacon's essay on
truth remind us that it is not only in moments of tranquillity
that philosophy dawns. Pilate's question continues to haunt
us. Even if language aims at truth, does it ever reach its
target? And how do we know? We spontaneously think of

truth in terms of reality. A belief, thought or sentence is true if it corresponds to reality. But what is reality, and how do we know it? Here is one of the places where philosophy is apt to go in circles. My desk is part of reality; so too is the colour brown: but what of the brownness of my desk? What makes *that* a part of reality? Surely, the fact that my desk is brown. Wittgenstein wrote that 'the world is the totality of facts, not of things.' (*Tractatus Logico-Philosophicus*, 1.1.) What makes it true that my car won't start is not my car, which is quite innocent in the matter, but the fact that my car won't start. Propositions are made true by facts, and each true proposition *identifies* the fact that makes it true. Only by dividing reality into facts, do we arrive at the entities to which true propositions correspond.

But what precisely *are* facts? And how does one fact differ from another? What is the fact that makes it true that my car is red? Surely, the fact that my car is red. There are as many facts as true propositions, and vice versa. But in that case, what is the difference between them? Why speak of truths *and* facts, when one and the same thing – a proposition, introduced by the word 'that' – is used to identify both of them? Why assume that facts exist, independently of the truths that express them?

But are we forced to identify facts through propositions? Do we not have ways of attaching our words to the *world*, for example, by pointing to what we mean? Could I not show what it is, that makes it true that my car is red, by pointing to the redness of my car? Well yes; but pointing is a gesture, and its meaning must be understood. Suppose I point my finger at the car. What leads you to suppose that I am pointing at the *car*, rather than the house behind my shoulder? After all, you could have read the gesture in another way, from the finger back to the shoulder. The simple answer is that we read the gesture as we do because there is a *rule* or *convention* which guides us. This is how we understand it. Moreover, the convention says only that the gesture points to the *thing* in front of me; further conventions have to be invoked, in order to know which *fact* about the thing I am singling out for your attention. Pointing belongs to language, and leans on language for its precision. It is only when we are able to read the gesture as an expression of thought that we can use it to anchor our words in reality. But that raises the question *what* thought? Why, the thought that my car is red! Indeed, no other thought would do: only this would serve to convey the fact that we have in mind, when referring to whatever makes it true that my car is red. We are once again back where we started. All attempts to pass from a thought to the reality described by it come round in a circle. The path from thought to reality leads in fact from thought to thought.

This is not surprising, according to Hegel: since thought is all there is. Or rather, not thought exactly, but something called 'spirit' (*Geist*) of which thought is the conscious expression. The difficulties over the concepts of truth and reality disappear, just as soon as we adopt the position of 'absolute idealism'. This tells us that the world is not some inert array of facts, standing outside and opposed to thought as its passive target, but thought itself, made real and objective through its own internal energy. If we wish to speak of the 'truth' of a thought, then we should use this term to refer, not to its correspondence with some unthinking reality, but to its coherence with the *system* of thought which identifies the world.

Surprising though it may seem, the dispute that I have just sketched, between the correspondence and the coherence theories of truth, continues unabated. Although expressed in different terms, it remains a real force in intellectual life, even among, perhaps especially among, those who do not really engage in it. The French writer Michel Foucault has invented a new way of doing history, based on the assumption that the truth of a thought is conferred by the system of ruling ideas. The concepts, theories and rationality of an epoch are those dictated by 'power'; there is no criterion against which to assess them, save those of some rival power which 'challenges' their ascendancy. Foucault tells us (in *Les Mots et les choses* (1966)) that man is a recent invention, and we are understandably startled. Does he mean there were no men around in the Middle Ages? No; he means that the concept: man – as opposed to gentleman, soldier, serf, judge, or merchant – has been current only since the Enlightenment. The implication, however, is that the concept creates what it describes, and that the theories of human nature which burst upon the world in the eighteenth century were theories which created the thing over which they disagreed. Until that time, there was *no such thing* as human nature.

All such ideas depend on the observation, in Wittgenstein's words, that you cannot use language to get between language and the world. Every time you describe reality, you use words; so every time you match a concept with the world, you are really matching a concept with a concept. You are picking out the objects referred to, and using concepts to do so. But this is necessarily so, as the case of pointing illustrates. You cannot pick things out unless you distinguish them from other things, and to distinguish one thing from another is to classify and therefore to apply a concept. Can it be that, from this trivial observation, such momentous conclusions follow, as that the world is nothing but thought, that there is no reality beyond concepts, or that man is a recent invention? Surely not.

The reason why those 'idealist' conclusions do not follow was given by Kant, in the first part of the *Critique of Pure Reason*. All thinking, he argued, depends upon the application of certain fundamental concepts or 'categories' – concepts like those of unity, substance, quantity, and causality, which are not arbitrary classifications but basic operations of thought. These concepts can be deployed only on the assumption of an independent reality: this assumption is built into them, along with the distinction between appearance and reality, seeming and being, which it is their role to elaborate. It is in their nature to 'aim beyond' experience to the world which explains it, and everyone who uses these concepts shares that aim, even the idealist who denies that he does so. Even he must use concepts of substance, causality, world and identity, if he is to say what he means; and these concepts commit him to the view that the world exists apart from his thinking.

So *does* the world exist apart from our thinking? Or do our concepts merely assume that it does? Kant's answer is ingenious. If we are to think at all, he argues, we must use concepts. If we use concepts we must deploy the categories. If we deploy the categories, we must assume the distinction between how things are and how they seem. If we make that distinction, we commit ourselves to an objective reality, and aim our discourse towards it. Even to deny the existence of reality is to think, and therefore to assume its existence. We do not need to argue that the world exists; its existence is presupposed in every argument, even the argument that it doesn't.

Kant produced many proofs of that kind, which attempt to show how we must think if we are to think at all. Such proofs go *beyond* rational deduction, to explore what it presupposes. Kant described them as 'transcendental', and his own philosophy as 'transcendental idealism'. A transcendental argument starts from a premise like 'I think,' 'I believe myself to be free,' or 'I have the idea of myself'; it then asks, 'What must be true if there is to be such a thought? What else must I think, and what must the world be like in which I exist, thinking such a thought?'

Kant's insight can be approached in another way. Foucault's conclusion about human nature stems from a failure to distinguish two kinds of concept: concepts which *explain* the world, and concepts which focus our response to it. The concept: fish is of the first kind; the concept: ornament of the second. When we divide the world into fish and not-fish, we do not regard this as an arbitrary expression of our *interest* in fish. We believe we are grouping things which belong naturally together, even if we don't know why. The classification is the first step in a *theory*, which does not merely describe the class of fish, but also explains it. The concept is *exploring* the world. At a certain stage we might discover that things which we once classified as fish are not fish at all, since they do not belong with the rest of the kind. This happened when whales were discovered to be mammals.

Ornaments have only one thing in common: namely, that we use them as ornaments. Our interest forms the class, and the concept and the interest arise and decline together. In an age when people do not distinguish between things which are, and things which are not, ornamental, there are no ornaments. It is perfectly reasonable to conclude, from the fact that the concept of an ornament is a recent invention, that ornaments too are recent inventions. No such reasoning could prove that fish are a recent invention. Concepts like those of fish and man are aimed at reality: they are forensic concepts, tied to explanation, and therefore to the Kantian categories. Their application is determined by the world, not by us, and they lead us on a voyage of discovery. Man could not be a recent invention, even if it is only recently that we have begun to use the concept. For the concept identifies something which preceded its own invention, whose nature is given by laws that have yet to be discovered. In such a case it is not the concept which creates the kind, but the kind which creates the concept. Men form what John Stuart Mill called a 'natural kind', as do fish, fleas and water.

Philosophy exists only because of the question 'Why?';

Why-questions arise in the context of rational discussion; rational discussion requires language; language is organised by the concept of truth; truth is a relation between thought and reality and reality is objective: neither created by our concepts, nor necessarily well described by them. Such is the train of thought that we have followed. So how do we know that our beliefs are *true*? Kant's argument shows that certain assumptions are unavoidable. But does that establish their truth?

3

The Demon

Many philosophers think not. An assumption may be both unavoidable and unjustified – like the assumption of honesty in a market. Perhaps the same is true of the assumption that our world is real. Consider the following argument, due to Descartes. An evil demon has control of my experience, and induces all my sensations, thoughts and perceptions, so leading me to believe that I inhabit an objective world. The demon's deception is systematic: at no point does the experience that he produces deviate from the norm that is familiar to you and me. But the world in which I believe myself to reside is a fiction; I am alone in the universe, with the demon who delights in deceiving me. How, in the face of this possibility, can I be sure that the world of my perception really exists, and really is as I think it to be?

This famous argument set modern philosophy on its sceptical journey. It does not merely point to the gap between appearance and reality. It adds that all methods we have for crossing this gap – perhaps all conceivable methods – fail to achieve their purpose. Locked within my illusory experience, I apply the best of scientific tests, distinguish the true from the false among my impressions, develop theories which refer to an underlying reality, and reassure myself, by reading Kant, that the world is there and I am a part of it. But all the while my thought, while imagining that it has ventured forth on a voyage of discovery, has merely patrolled its own perimeter, like a prisoner in a painted cell, who takes the pictures for windows. For all I know, there is nothing beyond my inner life, save the demon who produces it.

Someone could accept Descartes' argument as showing that, in the last analysis, the world remains hidden from us, lying beyond the boundaries of thought, but nevertheless believe that the distinctions between the true and the false, the real and the imaginary, the objective and the subjective, are genuine and useful. For, in an important sense, the hypothesis of the evil demon leaves everything unchanged. Whether the hypothesis is true or false, my experience will remain unaltered: indeed, that is the whole point of the story. So too will my concepts, my methods for distinguishing appearance and reality, and the process of scientific discovery which enables me to predict new experiences from old.

This is an important observation, since many current forms of scepticism give global arguments for local conclusions. Foucault's argument, considered in the last chapter, is one of them. It assumes that a general attack on the idea of 'correspondence' can be used to show that particular beliefs about the world (for example, that human nature is a constant datum) are false. But such general arguments show nothing of the kind; for they are *too* general. They do not disestablish the distinction between proven truths and mere opinions. For this is a distinction that is made *within* our scheme of thinking, and relies on no metaphysical picture. A similar instance is provided by 'deconstruction', the fashionable philosophy which tells us that, because we cannot use language to think outside language, we can never guarantee the meaning of our words. Hence there is no such thing as meaning, and the decision to attach a particular meaning to a text is always in some sense arbitrary, dictated by politics or power and not by the text itself. This too involves an illegitimate passage from a global theory to a local conclusion. Even if the global theory is true, it leaves everything at the local level unchanged. We still have criteria for distinguishing the meaningful from the meaningless; we still use these criteria in dialogue, and must do so if we are to think or speak at all. And we can still distinguish the true meaning of a text from the private associations of its reader.

The point is that global arguments of the kind advanced by Descartes set the world so far beyond our knowledge as to leave our concepts unaffected, including the concept of the world. If Descartes is right, then that which he is calling the world is not the thing that *we* know as world. The world for us is *our* world. It is identified within experience, by using methods intrinsic to human reason. Since these are the only methods we possess, it is futile to reject them. Besides, this rejection undermines the critical task, which is to define the areas in which the distinctions between appearance and reality, and objective and subjective, make sense.

This is very important when we come to moral thinking. Many people argue that moral judgements are subjective, perhaps even that they are 'relative' to the customs of a given community, or to the desires of its members. But it would be a very bad argument for this conclusion that *all* our judgements are subjective. From the philosophical point of view, what matters are the distinctions between moral judgements on the one hand, and scientific theories on the other. Even if morality and science are in the same boat, judged from the perspective of the evil demon, they are not in the same boat when judged from *our* perspective. We want to know whether *we* can make use of methods which will decide moral questions, in the way that we can decide scientific questions, without relying on unjustified prejudice.

The same goes for the interpretation of works of art.

'Deconstruction' tells us that there is no such thing as objective meaning, since meaning is the product of interpretation, and interpretation is always misinterpretation. Many critics seize on this global scepticism about meaning as a basis for denying that one work of literature can be more meaningful than another. There is no special reason to teach Shakespeare rather than Donald Duck or Barbara Cartland, when objective meaning attaches to none of them. Such a conclusion is quite unwarranted. Even if all our interpretations fall short of establishing an objective meaning – the meaning of a text in God's perspective – we could not interpret texts at all, if we made no distinction between plausible and far-fetched readings, between expressive and inexpressive uses of words, between penetrating and shallow descriptions. The criteria that we use in making these distinctions are forced on us by the very enterprise of reading literature, and remain unaffected by the claim that there is no access to the 'transcendental signified' – to the meaning behind the text, which only God could know.

Can we rescue the world from the demon? Or must we renounce the hope of proving that the world is really there, independently of our thinking? The answer depends upon our view of philosophy. Just how far can philosophical argument reach? Could philosophy ascend to the absolute perspective, the perspective which transcends the limitations imposed by human experience? Could thinking reach beyond itself, so as to light on the 'transcendental object' or 'thing in itself'? Those are the questions posed by Kant in his great *Critique of Pure Reason*. We have an image of what they mean – the image already offered to us, in Descartes' fantasy of the evil demon. But is it any more than an image? Phrased thus abstractly, is the question whether our world is real a real question?

Before venturing on an answer, we should pause to consider the nature of philosophical, as opposed to scientific,

truth. We divide truths into the contingent – those that
might have been otherwise – and the necessary. It is contingently true that London is the capital of England,
necessarily true that the capital of England is a town. Necessary truth is a difficult idea, but one fundamental to
philosophy. Indeed, on one reading of the subject, philosophy *deals* in necessary truths. Contingent truths, it is
said, are the province of science; they cannot be established
by pure reasoning, but only by observation and experiment.
But philosophy has no other method than pure reasoning at
its disposal. So if it comes up with results, they will not be
contingent, but necessary, like the truths of mathematics.
How can this be so? Philosophers have suggested various
answers to that question. One is to say that necessary truths
are in some sense *created* by our thinking. For example, we
use the word 'capital' in such a way that only towns can be
capitals – not villages, houses, trees or people. This is a
convention, a rule governing the use of a word. We could
have chosen another rule; but given this one, we are compelled by our own decision to conclude that 'The capital of
England is a town' must always be true. Necessary truth is
what the American philosopher W.V. Quine has called 'truth
by convention'. Other theories have been developed along
these lines. For example, it is sometimes argued that we
'construct' mathematical truths in the course of proving
them. The necessity of these truths stems from the fact that
they arise automatically from the rules of proof, and refer to
no independent reality.

Needless to say, such explanations are contentious at
best, and are never more contested than when applied to the
results of philosophy. Kant distinguished 'analytic' from
'synthetic' truths, the first being true by virtue of the meanings of words (for example, the truth that the capital of
England is a town), the second being true by virtue of some
independent reality. And synthetic propositions, he argued,

are not all contingent. Some are also necessary. He added that necessary truths cannot be proved by observation or experience, which only tells us how things are, never how they must be. Necessary truths are known, if at all, *a priori*, in other words by pure reasoning. We can understand how there can be truths which are analytic and *a priori*. But can there be synthetic *a priori* truths? This, he said, is the fundamental question of philosophy. For it is only by *a priori* reasoning, that philosophy could reach beyond the confines of human thought, so as to prove that the world is real.

Certainly no amount of science, and no amount of observation, will rescue us from the demon. Only an *a priori* argument will suffice; and it must have the 'transcendental' character suggested by Kant. It must examine what is presupposed by scepticism itself, in order to show that scepticism is refuted by its premises. Does such an argument exist?

4

Subject and Object

Descartes' argument about the demon is a splendid example
of a device much used in modern philosophy – the 'thought
experiment', in which a hypothetical state of affairs is invented in order to cast light on the nature and limits of
human knowledge. At the heart of the argument is the
distinction between myself and the 'external' world. My
experiences, perceptions and sensations belong to the 'inner'
realm; and they serve for me as signs of an 'outer' realm
whence, I suppose, they originate. I know them as mine, and
they belong with the things that I cannot doubt, not even if
the demon hypothesis is true. For example, I cannot doubt
that *I* exist; nor can I doubt that this perception, this sensation and this thought are occurring now in me. All 'external'
things are dubitable, but not those things which are the
present contents of consciousness, and which I know immediately as mine. It is as though the world were divided in
two: the closed, illuminated world of the self; and the undis-
covered country which lies in darkness all around.

   This picture has played a central role in modern philosophy, but took on a 'modernist' character after Kant,
becoming the central icon in a new religion – the religion of
'German classical philosophy', as it is called, for which 'German romantic philosophy' would be a more fitting name.
The founder of this religion was J.G. Fichte (1762-1814),
though his immediate followers, Schelling and Hegel, were

quick to take the credit. Fichte's way of arguing looks, in retrospect, very strange and is radically misrepresented by any attempt to provide a lucid summary, lucidity being the enemy of religion. Nevertheless, here is – very roughly – what Fichte said.

Philosophy must discover the 'absolutely unconditioned first principle of human knowledge' – i.e. the principle on which all knowledge can rest, but which itself rests on nothing. Logicians offer us an instance of necessary truth in the law of identity: A = A. But even that law presupposes something that we have yet to justify, namely the existence of A. I can advance to the truth that A = A, only when A has been 'posited' as an object of thought. But what justifies me in positing A? There is no answer. Only if we can find something that is posited in the act of thinking itself will we arrive at a self-justifying basis for our claims to knowledge. This thing that is posited 'absolutely' is the I; for when the self is the object of its own thinking, that which is 'posited' is identical with that which 'posits'. In the statement that I = I we have reached bedrock. Here is a necessary truth that presupposes nothing. The self-positing of the self is the true ground of knowledge. All knowledge begins from self-knowledge, and the self is the centre of its world.

Here begins the peculiar twist to Fichte's argument. What I 'posit', he argues, is an *object* of knowledge, and an object is not a subject. To have determinate knowledge of the subject is impossible: the self knows itself as subject only 'immediately' – that is to say, without concepts, so that nothing can be said about *what* is known. To have determinate knowledge of the self as subject would be like seeing the point of view from which you see the world. The subject is 'transcendental': it lies at the perimeter of the world, observing but unobservable. Hence that which comes before me in determinate self-knowledge is understood as not-self. The self is known in two ways – immediately, as self; and 'deter-

minately', as not-self. However, whatever lies in the not-self
is posited by the self – it has been translated from subject to
object, so as to make itself known. It is as though self-consciousness were traversed by a movable barrier: whatever
lies in the not-self has been transferred there from the self.
But since the origin of both self and not-self is the act of
self-positing, nothing on either side of the barrier is anything, in the last analysis, but self. In the not-self, however,
the self is passive. As such it can be organized by concepts
of space, time and causality, so as to constitute the order of
nature. As subject, however, the self is active and also free,
since concepts do not apply to it, and nothing that it does can
be described as the effect of some cause.

The transference from self to not-self is also an 'alienation'
of the self in the not-self, and leads to a 'determination' of
the self by the not-self. This 'self-determination' (*Selbstbes-
timmung*) is the highest form of self-knowledge, achieved
through alienation, but leading at last to a supreme act of
'self-realization', in which subjective freedom becomes an
objective fact.

Self, self, self – you can sympathize with Schopenhauer,
who dismissed Fichte as the 'father of *sham philosophy*, of
the *underhand* method ...'. Nevertheless, Fichte bequeathed
to German philosophy a powerful drama, which runs as
follows: Underlying knowledge, yet outside its purview, is
the free and self-producing subject. The destiny of the subject is to know itself by 'determining' itself, and thereby to
realize its freedom in an objective world. This great adventure is possible only through the *object*, which the subject
posits, but to which it stands opposed as its negation. The
relation between subject and object is one of opposition:
thesis meets antithesis, and from their clash a synthesis
(knowledge) emerges. Every venture outwards is also an
alienation of the self, which achieves freedom and self-knowledge only after a long toil of self-sundering.

That drama, give or take a few details, remains unchanged in Schelling and Hegel, and remnants of it survive through Schopenhauer, Feuerbach and Marx, right down to Heidegger. What it lacks in cogency it amply supplies in charm, and even today its mesmerizing imagery infects the language and the agenda of Continental philosophy. The journey of the self, from primitive subject to 'realized' object, becomes the recurring theme of all philosophy, which is useful to us first and foremost because it offers such striking proof of our own position, as sovereign creators of the world in which we live. Descartes shut the self in its inner prison, and Fichte made the place so comfortable, that the self decided to stay there, rejoicing in its sovereignty over a world that is in fact no larger than itself.

Hegel called the philosophy that he inherited from Fichte 'objective idealism'. The world is 'posited' by the self, and is therefore entirely composed of 'spirit': hence the name 'idealism'. But the self achieves self-knowledge as an object of its own awareness – by realizing itself in the objective world: hence the description 'objective'. Is this an answer to Descartes' demon? Surely not; the objective world has not been saved from the demon, but merely painted on the prison wall. The whole method and vocabulary of the Fichtean drama seems to bind us more firmly to the self, as the be-all and end-all of knowledge. There is nothing in this world save self, and the very act of reaching out to others is only an elaborate way of staying locked inside.

Words like 'subject' and 'object', 'subjective' and 'objective', 'inner' and 'outer' are by no means self-explanatory. They suggest a picture, rather than a theory – a picture, however, which has dominated Western philosophy since Descartes. The mind, according to this picture, is essentially 'inner', revealed to itself alone, and connected only contingently with 'outer' circumstances. The subject (or 'self') has a peculiar privileged view of this inner realm. He knows his present mental states indubitably and immediately. He has no such privileged view of his physical states, or of the 'outer' world, in which his body moves as one object among others. Hence he can doubt the existence of the external world and all that is contained in it – including other bodies and other minds. In considering the relation between thought and reality he is considering not 'our thought' but 'my thought'. Maybe there are no other people: maybe only I exist, and what I take for other people are no more than paintings on the wall.

This 'Cartesian' picture was assumed by Western philosophy for three centuries. Kant attempted to refute it; so did Hegel; but both produced another version, with the 'transcendental subject' at the place where the 'Cartesian ego' had been. The decisive refutation came with Wittgenstein, whose argument against the possibility of a 'private language', published in the posthumous *Philosophical Investigations* (1951), changed the course of modern philosophy. The Cartesian ego fortifies itself against the demon with the famous *'Cogito ergo sum'* – 'I think therefore I am'. The Fichtean self muscles its way into existence by 'positing' the object of thought, and the division between self and not-self. Both believe they are thinking, and that they know what they mean by 'I' and 'not-I', 'subject' and 'object', 'self' and 'other'. But whence did this knowledge of meanings arise? Did they invent a private language in which to pass on to themselves the rumour of their own existence? Or did they borrow their concepts from some other source?

Wittgenstein imagines the following case:

Suppose everyone had a box with something in it: we call it a 'beetle'. No one can look into anyone else's box, and everyone says he knows what a beetle is only by looking at *his* beetle. Here it would be quite possible for everyone to have something different in his box. One might even imagine such a thing constantly changing. But suppose the word 'beetle' had a use in these people's language. If so, it would not be used as a name of a thing. The thing in the box has no place in the language-game at all; not even as a *something:* for the box might even be empty. No, one can 'divide through' by the thing in the box; it cancels out, whatever it is.

The Cartesian picture envisages the mind and mental processes as private to the person who possesses them: only he can really know of their existence and nature; others have to guess from his words and behaviour, which are at best the effects of mental processes, and not the things themselves. But if that is so, Wittgenstein suggests, we could not use the terms of our public language in order to identify and refer to the mind. Someone may use the term 'beetle' just as I do, even though there is, in his case, *nothing* in the box. Yet we both agree that he has a beetle, that 'beetle' is the correct description of what he has, and that in this respect, as in any other that can be expressed in our common language, he is just like me! So it cannot be the 'inner object', the 'Cartesian mental process', that we refer to in our language: it drops out of consideration as irrelevant, since its presence or absence makes no conceivable difference to anything we say.

The following reply might be made: maybe each of us has his own *private* language, in which he refers to the 'inner processes' which elude the public 'language-game'. This private language is one that only the speaker understands, since no one else can know the objects to which he refers in it. The speaker can always be sure that he is using the words of his language correctly, since he knows, without checking on the matter, whenever an 'inner process' occurs.

But is this so? How does he know that the 'inner process' which he now calls 'grodge' is the same as the one which occurred when last he used that word? What criterion does he use – what criterion *can* he use – to attach his words to the things described by them? Indeed, how does he know that this thing called 'grodge' *is* an inner process? Perhaps it is a sensation – where the word 'sensation' is used with its ordinary meaning? If so, grodge is not an 'inner process', since no word in the public language (including the word 'sensation') could conceivably refer to such a thing.

The argument deserves far more space than I can afford. But its vertiginous effect should already be apparent. In their different ways, Descartes and Fichte retreat into the one realm which seems to offer certainty: the 'inner' realm, knowable to self alone. They rescue themselves from the outer world, retrieving the precious gift of thought with which to light the inner chamber. But the gift dwindles to nothing as they close the door. They imagine that they know what they mean by 'I', 'think' and 'self'; but this is precisely what they cannot assume. All is darkness in that 'inner world', and who knows what resides there, or indeed, whether anything resides there at all? As Wittgenstein puts it: a nothing would do as well, as a something about which nothing can be said.

If we accept the private-language argument, as I am inclined to do, then important conclusions follow. First, we have an answer to the demon. The argument tells us to stop seeking for the foundations of our beliefs, and to step out of the first-person viewpoint, which asks always what *I* can know, and *how* I know it. It invites us to look at our situation from outside, and ask how things must be, if we are to suffer from these philosophical doubts. Surely, we can ask the questions 'Why?' and 'How?' only if we have a language in which to phrase them. And no language can refer to a sphere of merely private things. Every language, even one that I invent for myself, must be such that others too can learn it. If you can think about your thinking, then you must do so in a publicly intelligible discourse. In which case, you must be part of some 'public realm', accessible to others. This public realm is also an objective realm. Unlike the inner realm of Descartes or Fichte, it might be other than it seems; its reality is not exhausted by our own impressions; it is the realm of being to which true propositions correspond, and at which our assertions aim.

Moreover, we must reject the Cartesian picture of the mind, which derives entirely from a study of the first-person case – a study of what is revealed to me, as I cease to meditate on the 'external world', and turn my attention 'inwards'. We must recognize the priority of the third-person case, which sees the mind from outside, as we see the minds of others. This third-person viewpoint is necessary to us, since without it we could neither teach nor learn what words like 'mind', 'thinking', 'sensation' and so on refer to. Nor could we use those terms of animals, even though they behave in so many ways as we do: for in their case, there *is* no first person, no self, wrestling with the not-self until both are determined and defined. Yet surely they have minds?

Some would say, nevertheless, that there *is* an 'inner' realm, an aspect of mind which is hidden from all but the subject, an indescribable but all-important *something*, which only I can know, but which is the secret stuff of mental life. After all, pain is not the same as pain-behaviour, and the peculiar awfulness of pain – *what it's like* – is never known except by feeling it.

But is that true? Have you ever watched by a sick-bed, and said to yourself, 'What I am seeing here is only pain-behaviour; the awful reality is something else, something hidden, something that only he can know'? On the contrary: you have seen *exactly* how awful it is, and you could hardly bear the sight. But suppose nevertheless that there *were* this 'purely subjective' aspect to our mental states. Imagine a society of beings exactly like us, except that, in their case, the subjective aspect is lacking. Their language functions as ours functions, and of course there is nothing we can observe in their physical make-up or behaviour that distinguishes them from us. They even speak as we do, and say such things as 'You don't know what it's like, to have a pain like this.' Their philosophers wrestle with the problem of mind, what it is, and how it relates to the body, and some of them are even Cartesians. Is that an incoherent suggestion? No, because it describes the case that we are in.

We understand the mind not by looking inwards but by studying cognitive and sensory behaviour. And we cannot study this behaviour without noticing the enormous structural similarities between human and animal life. We can arrange mental life in a hierarchy of levels; a creature may exhibit activity of a lower level, without displaying the marks of a higher, but not vice versa. Intuitively, the levels might be identified in the following way:

1. The sensory. We have sensations – we feel things, react to things, exhibit pain, irritation and the sensations of hot and cold. Maybe animals such as molluscs exist *only* at this level. Still, this fact is enough for us to take account of their experience, even if we do not weep like the walrus as we scrape the raw oyster from its shell, and sting its wounds with lemon juice.

2. The perceptual. We also perceive things – by sight, hearing, smell and touch. Perception is a higher state than sensation; it involves not just a response to the outer world, but an assessment of it.

3. The appetitive. We have appetites and needs, and go in search of the things that fulfil them – whether it be food, water or sexual stimulus. We also have aversions: we flee from cold, discomfort and the threat of predators. Appetite and aversion can be observed in all organisms which also have perceptual powers – in slugs and worms, as well as birds, bees and bulldogs. But only in some of these cases can we speak also of *desire*. Desire belongs to a higher order of

mental activity: it requires not just a response to the perceived situation, but a definite belief about it.

4. The cognitive. It is impossible to relate in any effective way to the higher animals, unless we are prepared to attribute thoughts to them about what is going on in their environment. The dog thinks he is about to be taken for a walk; the cat thinks there is a mouse behind the wainscot; the stag thinks there is a ditch beyond the hedge and makes due allowance as he jumps. In using such language, I am attributing beliefs to the animals in question. To put it in another way: I am not just describing the animal's behaviour; I am also making room for an evaluation of it, as true or false – I am comparing its beliefs with reality, making use of the very same concept of truth in which all human thinking is grounded. The dog, cat or stag might well be mistaken. Furthermore, to say that such an animal has beliefs is to imply not just that it can make mistakes, but that it can also *learn* from them.

Learning involves acquiring and losing beliefs, on the basis of a changed assessment of the situation; it involves recognizing objects, places and other animals; it involves *expecting* familiar things and being *surprised* by novelties. An animal which learns adapts its behaviour to changes in the environment: hence, with the concept of belief come those of recognition, expectation and surprise.

Learning is therefore not to be thought of in terms of the 'conditioning' made familiar by behaviourist psychology. The process of conditioning – the association of a repeated stimulus with a 'learned' response – can be observed in forms of life that have not yet risen to the cognitive level. Conditioning involves a change in behaviour, but not necessarily a change of mind. It has been abundantly shown that the higher animals acquire new behaviour not merely by conditioning, but in innovative ways, taking short cuts to the right conclusion, making intuitive connections, swimming to a place which they had known only through walking, or recognizing with their eyes the prey that they had been following by nose.

When describing behaviour of this kind – cognitive behaviour – we make unavoidable reference to the *content* of a mental state: the proposition whose truth is in question. The terrier believes *that the rat is in the hole*, it is surprised *that the hole is empty*; it sees *that the rat is running across the floor of the barn*, and so on. In all such cases the word 'that' – one of the most difficult, from the point of view of logic, in the language – introduces the content of the terrier's state of mind. The use of this term is forced on us by the phenomenon; but once we have begun to use it, we have crossed a barrier in the order of things. We have begun to attribute what are sometimes called 'intentional' states to animals: states of mind which are 'about' the world, and which are focused upon a proposition. Intentionality introduces not merely a new level of mental life, but also the first genuine claim of the animals upon our sympathies and our moral concern. For it distinguishes those animals which merely react to a stimulus, from those which react to the *idea* of a stimulus. Animals of the second kind have minds which importantly resemble ours: there is a *view* of the world which is theirs, an assessment of reality which we ourselves can alter. It is therefore possible to relate to a creature with intentionality, as we do not and cannot relate to a creature without it.

This partly explains the great difference between our response to insects, and our response to the higher mammals. Although insects perceive things, their perception funds no changing store of beliefs, but simply forms part of the link between stimulus and response. If the stimulus is repeated, so too is the response, regardless of the consequences – as when a moth flies into the candle flame, not out of stupidity or heroism, but because this is what happens when it perceives the light. Moths learn nothing from this experience, and have no store of information as a result of their past perceptions. They end life as they began it, in a state of cognitive innocence from which no experience can tempt them.

By contrast, dogs, cats and the higher mammals have an understanding of reality which motivates their behaviour. They learn from their perceptions, and we can share parts of our worldview with them. We can even join with them in a common enterprise, as when a shepherd and his dog work side by side.

That digression served the purpose of reminding the reader that the mind ceases to be mysterious, once we see it as it should be seen, as part of nature. There are creatures who have minds, but who have no 'self', and neither the need nor the ability to launch themselves on the path of self-discovery. The mind cannot be the mysterious thing that philosophers have made of it, if it is the common property of so many innocent beings.

But what then distinguishes us from the other animals, and who or what are *we*? Such questions can best be answered through a study of intentionality. The creature with intentionality has a view on the world, and the concepts and classifications in which that view is founded. He is not merely part of the natural order: he has a world of his own, created in part by the concepts through which he perceives it. In our case, these concepts are expressed in language, and ordered by rational discussion. Animals suffer from no such disadvantage. Their world is entirely ordered according to their interests: it is a world of the edible, the drinkable, the dangerous, the comfortable, and the unreliable. There is no place in this world for 'if' or 'perhaps', no place for 'Why?', 'When?' or 'How?', no place for the unobserved, or the unobservable. All learning takes place within a framework of interest, and the gulf between appearance and reality never opens so wide, that the mist of doubt can rise from it.

For us, however, the distinction between the world as it is, and the world as we think it to be, is one that our own concepts force on us. Our emotions, perceptions and attitudes have intentionality: they are focused by thought, and formed in response to our classifications. But they can also be corroded by thought, when the classifications on which they depend seem merely arbitrary, interest-relative, or intellectually confused. The respect and awe that we feel for sacred things could hardly survive the demise of the concept of the sacred. Yet many people would dismiss that concept as a survival of the 'pre-scientific' way of explaining things. Intentionality introduces the problem which I surveyed in the first chapter: the fragility of the human world, in the face of the scientific understanding which seems to undermine it.

Philosophy, in its negative, 'critical' employment, can tell us whether our concepts are in order; but not whether our beliefs are true. And the best way to vindicate a concept is to show that a distinction can be made, between a true and a false application of it. Thus, there is an old dispute, made central to philosophy by Locke, concerning the nature of 'secondary qualities' – qualities like colours, which seem intimately tied to the way things appear to us, but connected only obscurely with the underlying reality. If you ask what redness really *is* you find yourself in a sea of difficulties. Perhaps all we can say, in the last analysis, is that redness is a way of appearing. Nevertheless, our beliefs about the colours of things may be true, even if the concepts used to express them are deviant. We can justify the distinction between true and false colour-judgements, and that is sufficient vindication of the concept of colour.

Other fragments of the human world can be saved in the same way. Consider the concept of justice. Marxism tells us that this is a piece of 'bourgeois ideology', which gains currency only because it is functional in a capitalist economy. In a similar way, at the beginning of Plato's *Republic*, the cynical Thrasymachus argues that justice is nothing but the 'interest of the stronger': the only function of the concept is to describe the forces and interests which prevail in the social order. It may sometimes look as though the concept of justice were entirely undermined by such theories, losing its status as an instrument of judgement. But the appearance is illusory. Marxist theories of ideology leave everything exactly as it was, and even if true, do nothing to undermine either our beliefs or the concepts used to express them. We can all agree that the concept of justice serves to stabilize the social order. It is therefore in the interest of those who benefit from social stability (among whom the propertied classes are prominent) that standards of justice be widely accepted and applied. But this does not discredit the concept of justice. For there is a real distinction that we have in mind, when we distinguish just from unjust actions. By showing that there is a difference between a true and a false claim of justice the philosopher vindicates the concept.

But there is a further argument that the philosopher can make. He can describe the impact of the concept of justice on human intentionality. The human world presents another *aspect* to the one who thinks in terms of justice, than it presents to the one who does not. The first sees the world in terms of rights and obligations; in terms of desert, reward and punishment. His emotional life takes on another and more social structure: in place of rage he feels anger and indignation, and acceptance in place of jealousy. The 'me' feeling retreats from the centre of his consciousness, and another, more elevated and more impartial viewpoint takes its place. The task of exploring this impartial viewpoint, and describing the kinds of thought and emotion that belong to it, could be called 'phenomenology': at least that would be a good use for a much misused word. Phenomenology, as I envisage it, traces the *a priori* connections between concepts whose role is not to explain the world, but to focus our emotions upon it. It describes the way the world appears to us; and shows how appearances matter.

The concept of justice is one among many which only human beings deploy. Why is this? What is it about human intentionality, that makes so vast a difference between the human world, and the world of animals? Biology tells us that humans are animals; so why do we give ourselves such airs?

Persons

Well, we don't in fact. Human behaviour has been 'de-moralized', dragged down from its sacred pedestal and dissected in the laboratory. The very 'third-person viewpoint' that banishes Descartes' demon, prompts us to do the work of a more serious devil. The most important task for philosophy in the modern world is to resurrect the human person, to rescue it from trivializing science, and to replace the sarcasm which knows that we are merely animals, with the irony which sees that we are not. Having set aside the self and its dear illusions, we find ourselves in the midst of an ancient controversy. What exactly is it, that distinguishes us from the other animals; and does it justify the investment that we have made in the idea and the ideal of humanity?

Plato and Aristotle described human beings as rational animals, identifying reason as our distinguishing mark, and implying that our mental life exists at an altogether higher level than that of the other animals. Later philosophers, including Aquinas, Kant and Hegel, endorse the suggestion, and it is one that is intrinsically appealing. But it is not easy to say what it means. Definitions of reason and rationality vary greatly; so greatly, as to suggest that, while pretending to define the difference between men and animals in terms of reason, philosophers are really defining reason in terms of the difference between men and animals. On *one* understanding at least, many of the higher animals *are* rational.

They solve problems, choose appropriate means to their ends, and adjust their beliefs according to the evidence of their senses.

Nevertheless, there are capacities which we have and the lower animals do not, and which endow our mental life with much of its importance. Unlike the lower animals, we have a need and an ability to *justify* our beliefs and actions, and to enter into reasoned dialogue with others. This need and ability seem to underlie all the many different ways in which we diverge from the lower animals. If we survey our mental life, and examine the many specific differences between us and our nearest relations, we seem always to be exploring different facets of a single ontological divide – that between reasoning and non-reasoning beings. Here are some of the distinctions.

1. Dogs, apes and bears have desires, but they do not make choices. (Aristotle emphasizes this in his ethical writings.) When we train an animal, we do so by inducing new desires, not by getting him to see that he should change his ways. We, by contrast, can choose to do what we do not want, and want to do what we do not choose. Because of this, we can discuss together what is right or best to do, ignoring our desires.

2. The beliefs and desires of animals concern present objects: perceived dangers, immediate needs, and so on. They do not make judgements about the past and future, nor do they engage in long-term planning. Squirrels store food for the winter, but they are guided by instinct rather than a rational plan. (To put it another way: if this is a project, it is one that the squirrel *cannot change*, no more than an ant could resign from his community and set up shop on his own.) Animals *remember* things, and in that way retain beliefs about the past: but about the past as it affects the present. As Schopenhauer argues, the recollection of animals is confined to what they perceive: it involves the

recognition of familiar things. They remember only what is prompted by the present experience; they do not 'read the past', but 'live in a world of perception'.

3. Animals relate to one another, but not as we do. They growl and feint, until their territories are certain; but they recognize no right of property, no sovereignty, no duty to give way. They do not criticize one another, nor do they engage in the give and take of practical reasoning. If a lion kills an antelope, the other antelopes have no consciousness of an injustice done to the victim, and no thoughts of revenge. In general, there is a pattern of moral judgement and dialogue which is second nature to humans, but which is foreign to a great many – perhaps all – other animals. If sometimes we think we discern this pattern, as in the social behaviour of baboons and chimpanzees, our attitude radically changes: and for very good reasons.

4. Animals lack imagination. They can think about the actual, and be anxious as to what the actual implies. (What is moving in that hedge?) But they cannot speculate about the possible, still less about the impossible.

5. Animals lack the aesthetic sense: they enjoy the world, but not as an object of disinterested contemplation.

6. In all sorts of ways, the passions of animals are circumscribed. They feel no indignation but only rage; they feel no remorse, but only fear of the whip; they feel neither erotic love nor true sexual desire, but only a mute attachment and a need for coupling. To a great extent their emotional limitations are explained by their intellectual limitations. They are incapable of the thoughts on which the higher feelings depend.

7. Animals are humourless and unmusical. Hyenas do not laugh, nor do birds truly sing; it is *we* who hear laughter in the hyena's cackle, and music in the song of the thrush.

8. Underlying all those, and many other, ways in which the animals fail to match our mental repertoire, there is the

thing which, according to some philosophers, explains them all: namely, the fact that animals lack speech, and are therefore deprived of all those thoughts, feelings and attitudes which depend upon speech for their expression. This is consonant with the view of Aristotle, whose word for reason – *logos* – also means speech. (An animal, Aristotle says, is *alogon*, which means both non-rational and without language.) Of course, animals often emit noises and make gestures which *seem* like language. But these noises and gestures lack the kind of organization which makes language into the remarkable and mind-transforming thing that it is.

When it is argued that animals are like us in one of the above respects – animals like the higher apes, who seem to have a sense of humour, or dolphins, who seem to communicate their desires and to act in concert – the arguments tend to imply that these animals are like us in the other respects as well. It seems impossible to mount an argument for the view that the higher apes can laugh, which does not also attribute to them reasoning powers, and maybe even language (or at least, the power to represent the world through symbols). It is an empirical question, whether apes are like this, or can be trained to be like this; but it is a philosophical question, whether the capacities that I have described belong together, or whether on the contrary they can be exemplified one by one. It is my considered view that they do indeed belong together, and define a new and higher level of consciousness, for which 'reason' is a convenient shorthand.

But what exactly should we mean by consciousness? To many people consciousness is the essence of the mental, the feature which makes the mind so important to us, and the extinction of which is inherently regrettable, in a way in which the extinction of life (the life of a plant, say) is not. Descartes denied that animals are conscious, since consciousness, for him, was entirely bound up with the process of self-conscious reflection. But surely it is obvious that animals *are* conscious. This is proved by the fact that they are sometimes, but not all the time, *un*conscious. When asleep, anaesthetized or knocked out a dog is not conscious, as he is when alertly running about the garden. To describe a dog as conscious is to imply that he is aware of his environment, responds to it, learns from it, and is sentient. There is consciousness, in the sense of awareness, whenever behaviour must be explained in terms of mental activity. The dog has the kind of consciousness exhibited by his mental repertoire – which means that he is conscious as dogs are conscious, but not as bees or humans are conscious.

We should be careful, therefore, to distinguish consciousness from self-consciousness. Human beings are aware of themselves and their own states of mind; they distinguish self from other, and identify themselves in the first person. They knowingly refer to themselves as 'I', and are able to describe their own mental states for the benefit of others as well as themselves. This is what we should mean by self-consciousness, and it is a feature of our mental life which seems not to be shared by the lower animals.

Someone might ask how you could possibly know such a thing? Who am I, to decide that my dog has no conception of himself, no consciousness of him*self* as distinct from his desires, beliefs and appetites? The answer is that it is redundant to assume otherwise. We can explain the dog's behaviour without recourse to such an hypothesis, and therefore we have no grounds to affirm it. We can justifiably attribute to animals only the mental repertoire which is needed to explain how they behave. The situation never arises which will compel us to describe a dog's behaviour in terms of a conscious distinction between self and other, or between the world from *my* point of view, and the world from *yours*. Always we can make do with simpler assumptions –

assumptions about beliefs and desires, in which the 'I' concept has no role.

We should reflect at this juncture on the way in which a creature's mental horizon is broadened by language – by the ability to represent the world through signs.

1. Language expresses thoughts about absent things, about past and future things, about generalities, probabilities, possibilities and impossibilities. It emancipates thinking from the here and now, and causes it to range freely over the actual, the possible and the impossible. We attribute beliefs to the lower animals; but without language, these beliefs seem to be confined to the here and now of perception.

2. Language permits the construction of abstract arguments. It is the primary vehicle of reasoning, and the means to justify and criticize both beliefs and attitudes.

3. Hence language permits new kinds of social relation, based in dialogue and conversation. It enables people to criticize each other's conduct, to provide reasons to each other, and to change each other's behaviour by persuasion. Thus arises the practice of reason-giving, immediate offshoots of which are interpersonal morality and the common law.

4. Language expands the horizon of knowledge, and contains the seeds of scientific inference. But it also expands the *emotional* horizons. The emotions of animals, like their beliefs, concern present circumstances. A dog may pine away in its master's absence, and many of the higher animals form deep attachments. But even these endearing emotions are founded in familiarity, recognition and day-to-day habit. No animal is able to fear some hypothetical event; to envy, esteem or cherish an individual whom he has never met; to feel jealous over his mate's past or apprehensive for her future.

There are also emotions which are outside the repertoire of animals, for the reason that only a language-using creature could formulate the thoughts on which they depend. Thus indignation, remorse, gratitude, shame, pride and self-esteem all depend upon thoughts which are unavailable to creatures who cannot engage in reason-giving dialogue. Indignation is a response to injustice, and injustice in turn a concept which only language-users have. To cut a long story short, the higher emotions – those on which our lives as moral beings most critically depend – are available only to those who can live and think in symbols.

Much in philosophy is controversial. But I doubt that any philosopher who has studied the argument of Hegel's *Phenomenology of Spirit*, or that of Wittgenstein's *Philosophical Investigations*, would dissent from the view that self-consciousness and language emerge together, that both are *social* phenomena, and that the Cartesian project, of discovering the essence of the mental in that which is private, inner and hidden from external view, is doomed to failure. Moreover, most philosophers would agree that language requires an elaborate social stage-setting – if Wittgenstein is right, nothing less than a shared form of life, based in a deep consensus, will suffice. It is possible that animals could be granted honorary membership of this form of life – like the unfortunate chimpanzee called Washoe, lifted from her natural innocence in order to compete with humans on terms which humans alone define. But there is no evidence that the animals, left to their own devices, can achieve the particular form of social interaction required by language. And the efforts of Washoe have never satisfied the sceptics. Crucial elements of symbolic behaviour – syntactic categories, logical connectives, the distinction between asserted and unasserted sentences, between the passive and the active voice, the logic of modality and tense – fail to emerge, and in their absence it can reasonably be doubted that the ape has achieved true linguistic competence. *Maybe* she has. But the missing components are precisely those which endow language with its infinite elasticity, its ability to express thoughts beyond the present perception, to embed one thought within another, to entertain a thought without asserting it, to link thoughts in chains of hypothesis and argument, and to multiply thoughts indefinitely, so as to present a comprehensive picture of reality, as something independent of my own interests and desires.

The facts to which I have been pointing could be described in another and more pregnant way, by saying that human beings are persons. The concept of the person, which we derive from Roman law, is fundamental to all our legal and moral thinking. It bears the meaning of Christian civilization and of the ethic that has governed it, as well as the seeds of the Enlightenment vision which put Christianity in doubt. The masterly way in which this concept was lifted by Kant from the stream of social life and set upon a metaphysical pedestal should not distract us from its everyday employment, as the concept through which human relations are brokered. Our relations to one another are not animal but personal, and our rights and duties are those which only a person could have.

Human beings are social animals; but not in the way in which dogs, horses and sheep are social animals. They have intentions, plans and schemes; they identify themselves as individuals, with a unique relation to the surrounding world. They are, or believe themselves to be, free, and their choices issue from rational decision-making in accordance with both long-term and short-term interests. Although other animals are individuals, with thoughts, desires and characters that distinguish them, human beings are individuals in another and stronger sense, in that they are self-created beings. They *realize* themselves, through freely chosen projects, and through an understanding of what they are and ought to be.

At the same time, human beings live in communities,

upon which they depend not only for their specific ambitions and goals, but also for the very language with which to describe and intend them. Hence there is a permanent and immovable possibility of conflict, of a kind that does not occur in the animal kingdom. People depend on others, and also need to be free from them. Freedom means conflict; community requires that conflict be peacefully resolved. Hence negotiation, compromise and agreement form the basis of all successful human communities.

The concept of the person should be seen in the light of this. It denotes potential members of a free community – a community in which the individual members can lead a life of their own. Persons live by negotiation, and create through rational dialogue the space which their projects require. Such dialogue can proceed only on certain assumptions, and these assumptions show us what persons really are:

1. Both parties to the dialogue must be rational – that is, able to give and accept reasons for action, and to recognize the distinction between good and bad reasons, between valid and invalid arguments, between justifications and mere excuses.

2. Both parties must be free – that is, able to make choices, to act intentionally in pursuit of their goals, and to take responsibility for the outcome.

3. Each party must desire the other's consent and be prepared to make concessions in order to obtain it.

4. Each party must be accepted as sovereign over matters which concern his very existence as a freely choosing agent. His life, safety and freedom must therefore be treated as inviolable, and to threaten them is to change from dialogue to war.

5. Each party must understand and accept obligations – for example, the obligation to honour an agreement.

Those assumptions can be expressed in another way, by saying that human communities are composed of persons, who have rights, responsibilities and duties, and who endeavour to live by agreement with their fellows. If we do not recognize another's rights, then our relation to him is one of antagonism or war. If we do not feel bound by obligations, then we exist outside society and cannot rely on its protection. And in all negotiation, we must recognize the freedom, rationality and sovereignty of the other, if the outcome is to be acceptable to him and binding on both of us. All this is neatly summarized in the categorical imperative of Kant, which in its second formulation tells us that human beings are to be treated as ends, and never as means only: in other words, their freedom and rights are to be respected, and their agreement to be sought in any conflict. We can see the Kantian 'moral law' as consisting precisely in those rules which rational beings would accept, when attempting to live by agreement. These rules compose the quasi-legal part of moral thinking, and the concepts of right, obligation and personality gain their sense from them, just as the concepts of goal, foul and player gain their sense from the rules of football.

I shall return to the questions of morality. Before addressing them, however, we must face an awkward question. It seems that I am both an animal and a person. Moreover, I am the same animal today that I was yesterday; and also the same person. But could not these two ideas of identity diverge? Could not one and the same person migrate from body to body, and one and the same body incarnate now one person and now another? This, roughly speaking, is the problem of 'personal identity', and philosophers are no nearer to a solution to it than they were when it was first posed in its modern form by Aquinas. The modern question connects with a more ancient one: what happens to us at death? Granted that death is the end of the animal, is it also the end of the person who 'inhabits' him?

This is how I believe we should consider such questions.

Questions about identity are of two kinds: the real and the conventional. The question whether this is the same horse as George, whom I saw in this stable yesterday, is a real question: it is not for me, nor for us collectively, to *decide* that he is the same horse, and therefore to call him George. For the identity of a horse is determined by his nature: his being one and the same horse is the result of law-governed processes which do not depend upon *us* for their operation. In such a case we can make mistakes about identity, and the result may be disastrous. Someone who mistook this horse for George could end up in serious trouble, having been told that George is a safe horse to ride. The question whether this fence that I have just restored is the same as the one that stood here yesterday, is not a real question. I can settle it as I wish. Or, if something hangs on the answer – a question of legal ownership, for example, or of landlord's and tenant's responsibilities – we can collectively settle it by convention. There are many puzzles about identity which arises because we do not know whether it would matter, if we settled them by a decision. For example: is the Quarto version of *Hamlet* the same play as the Folio version? Is a car, all of whose parts have been replaced over the years, the same car as the one we started with?

At least one philosopher (Derek Parfit) has argued that the question of personal identity is not real, but conventional. It does not matter how we settle it, since it is not *identity* that interests us, in our relations with other persons and with our past and future selves. This seems to me to be quite wrong. The concept of the person exists because we relate to each other as individuals, and because the individuality of self and other is sacred in our dealings. Interpersonal relations depend upon rights and responsibilities which only individuals can have, and which extend over time. If we could not identify a person as one and the same at different times, then the practice of ascribing rights and duties would collapse; there would be no room for praise or blame, no basis for our moral emotions, and no point to moral dialogue. Emotions such as love, anger, admiration, envy and remorse, which posit personal identity as an immovable fact, would vanish, and with them would vanish the purpose of our life on earth.

Real questions of identity, however, must be dealt with in the same way as other real questions: from the third-person point of view. You cannot settle them by looking inwards, in search of the 'self' which remains one and the same in all its dealings, revealing itself to itself alone. For you could imagine this Fichtean self changing from moment to moment, being now one self, now another, and yet nobody (including itself) being any the wiser. It makes no conceivable difference whether you describe the self at one time as the same as, or different from, the self at another. The concept of identity loses its point, when applied to such a thing.

The point of the concept is in regulating our personal relations. Through our dealings with each other we lift one another into a higher realm, where the individual is seen as unique and irreplaceable, as the bearer of rights and duties which are his alone, and as the object of affections and judgements which single him out from all conceivable competitors, and focus exclusively on him. It is not convention which has determined the criteria of personal identity, but necessity. We determine the identity of a person by the very same procedures that we use to assign rights and liabilities – by asking who did this thing, who intended that, who is responsible for this and who allowed that. These are questions about reasoning, deliberating beings, and are settled by appeal to their memories, intentions, and undertakings, and not just by observing their bodily life. There is nothing in the nature of things to forbid the divergence of personal from animal identity: but if it happened often, we should have a different conception of human life.

The first-person perspective complicates things, since it causes us to entertain strange and unruly thoughts. When considering my own identity through time, the 'I' is always centre stage. What shall *I* do? What shall *I* feel or think? But this 'I' can be projected beyond death. I can wonder what I should think or feel, in the circumstances where my body lies inert and lifeless. Indeed, while I have no difficulty in imagining the death and dissolution of my body, I have a great difficulty in imagining the extinction of myself. I find it hard to think of a world without also thinking of my perspective upon it. And that means thinking of my own existence, even in a world from which my human life has gone.

These unruly thoughts have no real authority. Of course, I cannot imagine a world viewed from my perspective, from which the 'I' has gone. But the world doesn't have to be viewed from my perspective. Besides, what is this 'I'? Where in the world is it? Is it even *in* the world at all? Surely, the I is no more part of the world, than the retina is part of the visual field. The I is a point of view upon the world but not an item within it.

Death, Wittgenstein wrote in the *Tractatus*, is not part of life but its limit. He meant that we do not 'live through death', so as to emerge on the other side of it. Death is not an experience *in* life, and there is no such thing as looking back on death, and assessing it from some new perspective. This thought does nothing to allay human anxieties. However, it is not death that is the object of them, but finitude. It is the thought of our eventual non-existence that disturbs us – the thought that we exist only for a finite time. Schopenhauer wrote: 'A man finds himself, to his great astonishment, suddenly existing, after thousands of years of non-existence: he lives for a while; and then, again, comes an equally long period when he must exist no more. The heart rebels against this, and feels that it cannot be true.

The crudest intellect cannot speculate on such a subject without having a presentiment that Time is something ideal in nature.' Traditional religion consoles us with the thought of eternal life. Schopenhauer suggests another solution – not that we endure for an infinite time, but that we do not endure at all, since time is unreal.

Schopenhauer is right in thinking that it is time, not death, that troubles us. All creatures live in time; but self-conscious creatures also *situate* themselves in time, relating their past and their future to their present, and building time into the very idea of 'I'. In doing so, they become half aware of the treacherous guest they have invited in, and acquire the longing to expel him, to live in another world, a world outside time's dominion, in which the self will be free. Is this nonsense?

Time

Probably it *is* nonsense. But there is something unfathomable about time, and about the experience of being in it; people therefore feel cheated by any philosophy which leaves the matter unexplored. Aristotle says: 'One part of time has been and is not, while the other is going to be and is not yet. Yet time – both infinite time and any time you care to take – is made up of these. One would naturally suppose that what is made up of things which do not exist could have no share of reality.' To put the point in another way. If you subtract from time all the bits that are not, you are left only with the 'now': and not even with that, for no sooner are you left with it, and it has gone. Many other philosophers have followed Aristotle in thinking, both that the idea of the 'now' is essential to time, and also that this very fact casts doubt on time's reality. Time orders the world as past, present or future; yet each of these is, in its own way, unreal. The idealist philosopher J.M. McTaggart went further, arguing that temporal order is actually impossible, since every event contained in it would have to be simultaneously past, present and future, and these predicates directly contradict one another.

McTaggart's statement of the argument is more subtle than that; but the gist is clear. Time is unintelligible without the 'now'; and the 'now' is contradictory. One response is to say that nowness is not a property of an event, and that judged in itself the world contains no 'now': there is no past, present or future, but only 'before' and 'after'. Events can be ordered in time relative to one another, but no moment is privileged as 'now'. On this view 'now' is like 'this' or 'I': it expresses the point of view of the speaker, but not a feature of the world.

However, it is precisely the situation of the speaker which concerns us. Time would be no problem, if it were not for the fact that there are beings in time who are also conscious of time's passage. And there seems to be something that they are compelled to think about time, which they cannot put into words, unless it be words like 'then' and 'now'. True, there are those who refer instead to the river of time, adding that you can never step twice into any part of it; there are those who describe 'time's arrow', adding that it has no target, and comes from nowhere. But those metaphors hardly stand up to examination. There may be a certain uplift in singing 'Time like an ever-rolling stream bears all its sons away'. But this uplift comes from imagining time as a spatial process. And that is absurd, since processes occur in time, and that in which all processes occur cannot itself be a process.

There is a temptation to think of time in spatial terms. Modern physics makes use of a single geometry to describe 'space-time', with time as a fourth dimension. But physics refers only to the order of 'before' and 'after', and not to the 'now'; this 'geometrical' treatment therefore leaves out of consideration the matters which most disturb us. From any philosophical point of view, time is very different from space. First, it has direction: that is to say, it moves always from past to future, and never from future to past. This sounds clear, so long as you don't examine it too closely; hence St Augustine's famous remark: 'What then is time? If no one asks me, I know; if I wish to explain it to one who asks, I know not.' And we have already glimpsed part of the reason for St Augustine's hesitation. It is not time that has direction, but things *in* time. Nothing ever moves backwards in time. Nothing ever becomes earlier than it was. But that sounds like a tautology. Why, then, is it so mysterious?

Secondly, you cannot move through time, as you can through space. You are swept along by it. There is no way of hurrying forward to a future point at twice the speed of your neighbour; there is no lingering or dawdling by the way. The temporal order compels you to be exactly when you are at any moment, and nowhen else.

Thirdly, everything in time occupies the whole of the time during which it exists. You entirely fill one part of the temporal dimension. So too do your contemporaries. There is no jockeying for position in time, no pushing aside of its occupants. Nothing in time excludes anything else. Time does not have 'places' that are 'occupied'. We cannot therefore speak of a position in time, as we would a position in space. Times, unlike places, are not locations over which we can contest, or territories that we can claim. They are all-embracing and inexorable.

The difficulties over 'now' have led some philosophers to doubt that time as experienced is the same thing as physical time. Bergson, in his *Essai sur les données immédiates de la conscience*, distinguished *le temps* from *la durée*, arguing that while physics can study the first, it cannot know the second, since the character of duration is revealed only by the process of life – of *living through* the sequence of events. In living through events I acquire a knowledge of their inner order, of the way in which one thing grows from and supersedes another; and this knowledge is enshrined in memory. The remembered order is an order of meaning, in which the uniform flow of physical time is 'thickened' according to the subjective significance of events.

Bergson's thoughts, which were instrumental in inspiring Proust to write one of the greatest novels of our century, are really meditations on the 'now': lived time is time observed, time passing through the gateway of the 'now' into the tomb of memory. But that description is as misleading as Bergson's. It is not time that passes through the 'now', but events: and events retain their order of before and after, whether they are now or then. Why not discard the 'now', which belongs not to time but to our perspective, and regard *le temps*, physical time, the sequence of before and after, as all that there really is?

Such a dismissive solution does not satisfy us. The problem of time is, in the last analysis, the problem of our own *being* in time: the astonishment to which Schopenhauer refers stems from the fact that we are related in time to the things which we know and love, and therefore locked with them into the order of then and now. At any moment, our situation is exactly that described by Aristotle: everything that we cherish or fear, everything that matters in the least to us, has either vanished forever, or not yet arrived. All that we have is the infinitesimal fragment of the now, which vanishes in turn just as soon as we try to lay our hands on it.

Plato described time as 'the moving image of eternity'. He did not deny the reality of time; but he believed in another, timeless realm, which casts its shadow on the turning spheres below. This idea has recurred so often in philosophy, as to suggest that there is either truth in it, or a permanent need to believe so. Although philosophy is not religion, and stands in judgement over religion as over every other mode of thought, the philosopher was esteemed in antiquity as the purveyor of wisdom. And wisdom is worth nothing if it does not console. Plato's vision of that higher, timeless realm has soothed so many troubled souls in so many dire conditions, that we should treat it with the utmost respect, even if we cannot endorse it. The vision was adapted to Roman Stoicism by Cicero, to Christian devotion by St Augustine, and to pagan credulity by Plotinus. And when it visited the Roman philosopher Boethius (*c.* AD 480-524) as he lay in prison awaiting execution, he recorded it anew, in *The Consolation of Philosophy*, a luminous work which was treasured by poets, philosophers and theologians for a thousand years thereafter.

The traditional Platonic elucidation of the idea of the timeless and eternal is through mathematics, and through the contrast between durable objects and numbers. It is conceivable that a lump of rock should last through the whole of time; but it is essentially *in* time, and subject to change *over* time. If the number 2 exists, then it exists at every time; but it does not exist *in* time, since it takes no part in temporal processes, nor does it change. It possesses all of its properties essentially and eternally. Nothing ever *happens* to the number 2; nor does it cause anything to happen to anything else.

The ontological argument seems to imply that God, if he exists, is eternal in just that way. He possesses all his properties changelessly and essentially, and exists everywhere and everywhen only because he exists nowhere and nowhen. But if God is really *outside* time, how can he influence temporal processes? For instance, suppose God decides to flood the world. There is then something true of God at one time (namely, that he is flooding the world), that is not true of him at another. Furthermore, if God is related to the world (for instance, as its creator), then every change in the world will be a change in God's relational properties: he stands now in *this* relation to the created sphere, now in *that*. Yet, if God is eternal as the number 2 is eternal, no such thing could be true.

Similar problems arise when we consider our relation to eternity. How do I encounter that timeless realm, when existing in the here and now? Where and what is that 'point of intersection of the timeless with time', which Eliot described as the 'occupation of the saint'? If we encounter something in time, we know for certain that it is not the number 2; the same ought surely to be true of all eternal objects. And how is it possible to 'rise' to the eternal sphere, as Plato so beautifully describes the soul rising and freeing itself, in the *Phaedo* and the *Symposium*?

Spinoza's approach to these problems is in many ways the most illuminating. By his own version of the ontological argument, he proves that at least one 'substance' exists, and also that at most one substance exists: substance being infinite in every positive respect. (*Ethics*, Part I.) This one substance therefore embraces everything that is, and there can be no distinction in reality between God and the natural world. Either the natural world is identical with God (the one substance), or it is 'predicated of' him, as one of his 'modes'. (The terminology of 'substance and mode' was taken over by Spinoza from Cartesian philosophy: the distinction is roughly between that which is self-dependent and self-sustaining (substance), and that which depends on, inheres in, or is known through something else.) Spinoza argues for the identity of God and the natural world, and elects for the title 'God or Nature' (*Deus sive Natura*) as the correct name of the one thing that is everything.

On this view, the distinction between the creator and the created is not a distinction between two entities, but a distinction between two ways of conceiving a single reality. I can conceive the divine substance now as a whole, self-dependent and all-embracing, and now as the sum of its various 'modes', unfolding each from each in a chain of dependency. The first way of conceiving substance is like the mathematician's way of conceiving a proof: studying the timeless logical connections that deliver truth upon truth from a handful of all-embracing axioms. The conclusions of a proof are eternally 'contained in' the axioms, and made explicit in the proof of them: in some such way reality is 'contained in' God, and derivable from his eternal essence. The second way of conceiving substance is like the scientific image of the world, as something as yet unknown, but slowly yielding its secrets as we interrogate it through observation and experiment.

It is in terms of that intellectual contrast that Spinoza explains the distinction between eternity and time. The world can be conceived *sub specie aeternitatis* (under the aspect of eternity), as a mathematician conceives numbers and proofs; or *sub specie durationis* (under the aspect of duration), as ordinary people observe the sequence of events in time. There are not two realms, the eternal and the mutable, but again two ways of conceiving the one reality. To study the world *sub specie durationis* is to study it as it is; time therefore is real. Nevertheless, studying the world in this way, we can never grasp the whole of it: we can never reach the sum of those necessary connections, which show how each truth contains and is contained in every other. When, as in the ontological argument, we see the world *sub specie aeternitatis*, we see that what is, must be, and that all truth is necessary, eternal truth. Then, and only then, do we have an 'adequate' idea of the world.

In Spinoza's philosophy, everything less than the whole of things becomes a mode of that whole; all distinction dissolves, and individuals melt away into a vast unruffled sea of being, stretching without limit through eternity. Even if time is real, it has little authority in the philosopher's view of things. For the grid of duration – of 'before' and 'after' – divides the one substance in ways that make no sense from the supreme perspective upon them. To see how things ultimately are (to acquire an 'adequate idea' of the world) we must discard duration, and see reality under the aspect of eternity.

There is a price to be paid for this conception of the world, as Leibniz saw. Spinoza's philosophy lacks what medieval philosophers called the *principium individuationis* – the principle of individuation – which distinguishes one thing from another, which attributes identity and reality to the human subject, and which attaches our discourse to a realm of objective things. Such a principle requires the framework offered by space and time: we count the individuals in our world by locating them in space, and identifying them through change. We too are individuals. My destiny is of concern to me, precisely because there are things which happen to *me*. Without identity through time I could not regret the past; I could not plan for the future; and I could not wonder what will happen when I die. And without a position in space I could not act in this world: I could do neither good nor evil, but would be reduced to a state of passive contemplation, with reality drifting by me (although 'by' is the wrong word) as in a dream.

In the face of this, some might be tempted to follow Schopenhauer, who believed that whatever of me survives does so, not because it is me, but because it has ceased to be me or anyone, has shed all remnants of identity, and been reabsorbed into the primeval sphere of Will. Although Schopenhauer embellishes this thought with much intriguing metaphysics, it is hardly a consoling one. For it merely emphasizes the fact that my life is finite, that death is the end of me, and that whatever survives thereafter is nothing to me. To think away time is to think away myself.

Indeed, it is to think away the whole observable world. Kant described time as 'the form of inner sense', meaning that all our mental states are intrinsically ordered in time: I could never be conscious of a mental state as mine, without also being aware of it as *now*, and without relating it to what precedes and succeeds it. An object that existed outside time could not be an object of experience. Nor could it relate to the observable world. How therefore could something whose identity is bestowed by time exist *outside* time, and still be the same individual? Surely the suggestion is incoherent. Whatever can appear under the aspect of eternity is surely distinct from *this, here, now*?

Is that the end of the matter? Not quite, though to proceed further down this path is to enter a realm so dark that only silhouettes are visible. The point, emphasized by many modern philosophers, that objects are individuated through space and time, suggests that the same is true of me, and that I can identify myself only through my spatio-temporal co-ordinates. But this is not true. I may see a figure in a mirror and wonder whether it is me. In the normal case, however, I do not even have the *question* whether this, of which I am conscious, is me: I just know that it is. Whenever I identify myself as the *subject* of consciousness, rather than the object, then I do so without reference to a spatio-temporal framework, without criteria of identity, and without the possibility of error.

Furthermore, we are acutely aware of the distinction between subject and object, and when we encounter other subjects in the world of objects, we treat them in a special way. Suppose an apple falls on the table before me, and I ask the question 'Why?' The right way to answer is by citing a cause: it fell because the breeze dislodged it. By giving causal explanations we are automatically ordering events in space and time, and the causal relation itself is intrinsically temporal. (In general causes precede or are simultaneous with their effects.) But suppose that you throw an apple onto the table before me, and I ask the question 'Why?' As we saw in Chapter 1, the question now has quite another sense. In the normal case – that is, the case where it is not asked *of* you, but addressed *to* you – the question looks for a justifying reason, not a cause. Why should you throw this apple down before me? The answer might be that I deserve it, or that it would be good to eat.

Justifying reasons lead us in a new direction: not to other

events, related to this one by space and time, but to abstract principles of right. We find ourselves enunciating 'timeless' laws, which are not summaries of observation but prescriptions addressed to all rational beings. Consider the principle that everyone should receive what he deserves: this applies without reference to place or time, and concerns merely the situation of the subject, and his relation to other subjects like himself. It is as though subjects addressed one another from a point of view outside space and time – condemned to see one another 'under the aspect of eternity'. And this is how we see our own actions, when they proceed truly from us. If I do something that I regard as wrong, my reaction is one of shame or remorse. I carry the stain of this action around with me, and I feel myself to be judged. Judgement in such circumstances has a timeless character: it is always with me, inscribed hereafter in my very self, regardless of subsequent events.

This predicament of the self-conscious subject gives rise to a strange experience – an experience whose strangeness we notice only when compelled to philosophize. It is as though the world of objects were perforated by apertures, from each of which a subject peers, and through each of which we glimpse the 'transcendental' province of another's will. The eyes of a person may accuse, condone or exonerate. They do not look at things only: they offer glances, and summon other glances in response to them. Lovers' glances are an instance of what I have in mind. A lover shines his eyes into the depths of his beloved, calling the other subject to the surface: the world of objects falls away, and self presses to self at a common boundary. This experience is hard to describe in words, but here is a version due to Donne:

> Our eye-beams twisted, and did thred
> Our eyes, upon one double string;

> So to'entergraft our hands, as yet
>   Was all the meanes to make us one,
> And pictures in our eyes to get
>   Was all our propagation.

This experience takes place in time. But it is frequently described as timeless, as though it opened onto a sphere outside the natural order. And we can see why. For lover's glances are aimed at that which lies beyond the moment, beyond cause and effect, beyond the 'empirical' world. Maybe there is an illusion at work here. But it arises from our deepest thoughts about ourselves. In all our deliberations we are aware of this indescribable thing at the periphery of our mental vision: the subject who acts, who responds to reason, and who does not just show himself in the world of objects, but appropriates that world as his own.

The phenomena that I have just sketched do not prove that the individual can exist in a timeless state. But they suggest that there is something in our condition which invites us to think of ourselves in that way, rather as Spinoza thought of the world. On the one hand we are objects in the world of nature, bound by time, space and causality; on the other hand we are subjects, who relate to one another as though bound only by reason and its immutable laws. And our individuality is conferred by this *second* view of ourselves. The subject is unique, irreplaceable, the focus of those attitudes like erotic love, praise, accusation and remorse, which cannot be directed to something which is conceived merely as an object. And it is these attitudes which tell us what the individual really is, and why he matters.

But can we make sense of those ideas? Can we make sense of them, that is, without embracing a Cartesian or a Fichtean view of the self, as the *object* of its own awareness?

God

The short answer is that I don't know. But the next three chapters will help us to clarify the question. Much of modern philosophy leaves its readers cold because it begins from an impoverished conception of the human subject. We all know in our hearts, even if we have never put the matter into words, that the human subject is the strangest thing that we encounter; and when we do try to put the matter into words, we find ourselves employing concepts which we can hardly explain – such as: self, will, freedom, responsibility, individuality, transcendence. It is because they recognize these truths that philosophers in the Continental tradition – and especially romantics like Hegel and Heidegger – have acquired such a following; and it is because they seem to neglect them, or at any rate make no show of confronting them, that Anglo-American philosophers write, on the whole, only for each other, in journals that few people troubled by life's brevity are tempted to read. This is a great pity, for Anglo-American philosophy has much more to say to us than Marxism, phenomenology, existentialism, structuralism, or deconstruction (to name but a few).

Our most pressing philosophical need, it seems to me, is to understand the nature and significance of the force which once held our world together, and which is now losing its grip – the force of religion. It could be that religious belief will soon be a thing of the past; it is more likely, however, that beliefs with the function, structure and animus of religion will flow into the vacuum left by God. In either case, we need to understand the why and wherefore of religion. It is from religious ideas that the human world, and the subject who inhabits it, were made. And it is the ghostly residue of religious feeling that causes our most intractable philosophical problems.

Two distinct phenomena are involved in religion, as we know it: religious observance, and religious belief. These do not necessarily coincide. There are religions which remain vague or non-committal in matters of doctrine, while insisting on the most scrupulous observance. Thus, traditional Chinese religion lays great emphasis on rituals, from the exact performance of which our ancestors are supposed to benefit, while offering only the most rudimentary theological speculations by way of explaining how that could be so. Something similar could be said of Japanese Shintoism, and even of the religions of Greece and Rome. The anecdotal theology of Hesiod seems half-aware of its own metaphorical nature; by the time of Ovid the awareness is open-eyed and full of wonder – wonder not at the world of divinities, but at the poet's half-amused belief in them. Pious observance mattered more in ancient society than correct ideas about the supernatural beings who supposedly required it. By recognizing a changing multitude of gods, the Romans implied that it was of no great importance whether you actually believed in them. In those days you could even become a god, by means similar to those now used to obtain an earthly title. It is hard to believe that the average Roman took the gods very seriously, when his emperor could arbitrarily declare himself to be one of them. But this did not remove the respect for sacred things on which, to the Roman mind, civil order depended. It was still necessary to invoke the *lares et penates* (the household deities), to treat old age with reverence, and new life with awe. It was still necessary to consecrate the most important happenings – birth, marriage, death and membership – to something higher than one's own desire. Social obligations arose not from contracts only, but from solemn vows, and a kind of eternal jurisdiction was implied in this – as in the fate of 'pious Aeneas', as he departed forever from the flames of Troy.

Just as there can be religious observance without religious belief, so can there be belief without observance, or belief which leaves observance to the conscience of the believer. The Protestant tradition of Christianity has tended in this direction, gradually shedding what it regards as the idolatrous trappings of the Roman Catholic ritual, until little remains of the outward display of religion, and all is reduced to a stark confrontation between God and the soul. Such an attitude is fraught with dangers. The *via negativa* which leads to God by discarding the images that disguise him, may come close to discarding God as well – as in the negative theology of Karl Barth. In its war against the impure and the inessential, the Protestant religion is always in danger of negating itself: which is one reason why the Protestant churches are now in far greater crisis than the Church of Rome. Nevertheless, in its stable and historically durable forms, the Protestant religion has shown an interesting tendency to combine clear theological beliefs with utter vagueness in ritual and worship.

There is, it seems to me, a great mystery in the fact that rational theology should also be *religion*: that ritual observance, ceremony, and the sense of the sacred should come in time to have the God of theology as their object. The two things may certainly maintain separate lives in a single soul. Aristotle, for example, most lucid proponent of an abstract monotheism, comforted himself with the myths and customs of the Greek religion; while Muhammad, seized by the sublime conception of the one God, unearthly and all-transcending, nevertheless dutifully visited the sacred stone of the *kabbah*. But those are transitional cases, in which the light of monotheism had not yet swept away the mythic shadows. The belief in God, the prime mover and creator, who exists eternally and of necessity, who is 'cause of himself', whose essence it is to exist, and who is all-knowing, all-powerful and all-good: this belief immediately congeals with the ancient cults, which become cults of the supreme being. The interest that the ancestral ghosts and heroes maintain in their survivors becomes an attribute of God's. Amazingly, the First Cause himself, the unmoved mover, takes a personal interest in his creation and in the doings of all of us. The God of theology – that abstract entity which proves itself into existence by an argument which is obviously sophistical but which has never been conclusively refuted – becomes a person, and even (for a Christian) an incarnate person, bridging in his own divine essence the otherwise impassable barrier between the empirical world of our experience and the transcendental world of our belief. Spinoza saw an absurdity in this, rejected the idea of transcendence, tore away from God the veil of personality, rebuffed the suggestion that God should want our love or need our worship, and dismissed the myths and the sacred customs as so many 'graven images'. But Spinoza was denounced as the enemy of religion, the one who, in order to save theology, had sacrificed its purpose. For the mass of humanity there is no gap, and no contradiction, between theological belief and religious observance. Why is this? What is it that compels the one who believes in God the creator, who hopes for eternal life and trusts in a transcendental reality, nevertheless to worship only at the altar of his ancestors, living by customs that derive no endorsement from the revealed will of God, and perhaps looking on rival customs as horrendous acts of sacrilege? Why is it that our rational pursuit of an answer to the riddle of existence leads us *in the very same direction* as does the mythic consciousness, as does the sense of sin and defilement, and as do the customs and ceremonies that define an earthly community?

I see myself and others as objects in the world of nature; but I also see myself and others as subjects, in some way outside the natural order, looking into it from a 'transcendental' perspective. This division between object and subject is inescapable, and, as Hegel saw, the root cause of our estrangement. All our projects – all those that really matter to us – are framed in terms of the subject: it is the self which I try to capture in love and desire, and which always eludes me; and it is the self which I strive to realize in the objective world, for which I demand recognition and right, and which remains untouched by the tinsel honours that bedeck the human person. Nothing *in* the world can ever *be* a self: to think otherwise is to fall victim to an illusion of grammar. It is to deduce from the valid use of 'myself', that there is a self to which I refer. (This is like deducing the existence of a sake from the valid use of 'for my sake'. In one sense, 'What kind of thing is a sake?' is a paradigm of a philosophical question.)

To put it in another way: the rational being lives in a condition of metaphysical loneliness. He may not describe it in those terms – and it is very unlikely that he would use the Kantian idiom of my previous paragraph. But if he is self-conscious at all he will suffer the effects of this loneliness, and perhaps find consolation in the texts, from *Gilgamesh* to *Four Quartets*, which meditate on our fallen state, and on the gap between human longing and human satisfaction: the gap which comes from being not *of* this world, but only *in* it. The innocence of the animals consists in having no knowledge of this gap; it is our awareness of it that leads both to religious ritual, and to the belief in a transcendental deity: and these two come together because they are addressed to a single need.

Self-conscious beings do not unite in herds or packs; they come together in two quite different ways: first as communities regulated by negotiation, law and contract; secondly as tribes or congregations, united by a bond of membership. Anthropologists have long puzzled over the need for membership, over the rituals which establish it, and the penalties by which it is enforced. But almost all would agree with Durkheim's thesis, in his *Elementary Forms of the Religious Life*, that religious observance is, in its primitive form, part of the ritual of membership, and takes its sense from the new and 'sacramental' bond that is established when people adopt common myths, common liturgies, and a common distinction between the sacred and the profane. This sacramental bond should be understood in metaphysical terms. It is a bond between *subjects*, in a world of objects. Through religious observance people *enter together* into the sphere beyond nature. The function of ritual is to mobilize words, gestures and dances – those forms of behaviour which are replete with the experience of self – and to turn them in a supernatural direction. The rituals are essentially shared, and each subject, repeating the magic words, or performing the magic gestures, is freed for a moment from the world of objects, flowing freely into a 'mystic communion' with the other subjects who worship at his side. No ordinary commerce between people could achieve this effect, since ordinary commerce depends on negotiation, consent, and a respect for rights and duties, and therefore assumes the subject to be alone and inviolable in his sovereign territory, shut up in a fortress which he alone can occupy. The 'first-person plural' of the religious rite overcomes this isolation and creates, for a brief but necessary moment, the sense that we stand together outside nature, sharing the subjective viewpoint which otherwise we know only as 'mine'.

But the thought of this supernatural sphere gives rise to the idea of a transcendental perspective: a view which is not *from* the subject, onto the world of objects, but *onto* the subject, seeing the self as it truly is. This, I believe, is how the God of monotheism is conceived: as a self-conscious subject who confronts other subjects *directly*, and who allocates their place within the mystic communion. In the divine consciousness, subject and object are one; the divide between them is overcome and made whole. The religious ritual overcomes our loneliness; but without God this 'collective subjectivity' hovers on the verge of illusion. With God, the illusion becomes reality, subjectivity becomes another and higher objectivity, and we *take our place* in the realm where subjects are fully at home with each other and transparently known. We are not merely consoled, but redeemed, and this metaphysical redemption changes daily life. For, as I argued in the last chapter, the self-conscious being casts judgement on himself, and this judgement has a timeless character: it cannot be overcome in the world of objects, but only by an inner renewal, which removes the stain of guilt. Guilt remains just so long as subject and object are divided, the first standing in judgement over the second. But God, who sees subject as object, heals the rift between them, 'purifies' them of their common pollution, and launches them as one into the world of self-conscious choice.

The experience that I am trying to convey is familiar to all who partake of Holy Communion; it has been matchlessly dramatized by Wagner in *Parsifal*, and has received countless commentaries in works of devotion. But, with the notable exceptions of Hegel and his critic Kierkegaard, philosophers barely mention it. For most philosophers in our tradition, there is little more to the question of God than the flimsy proofs for his existence. If I am right, however, there is much more. For the impulse to believe, I suggest, stems from a metaphysical predicament. And the God of monotheism is the only possible solution to this predicament, the only thing which stands wholly outside nature, confronting us as a person, and raising us to the transcendental realm to which our aspirations tend.

It is therefore necessary to examine whether this personal God exists: this is a question of some urgency, if it is really true that the self calls out for him. Now, it is only when people began to wander freely among strangers that the gods of the tribe seemed inadequate to protect them. The 'God of the Philosophers' is therefore a late-comer; but the speculations about his nature have been surprisingly uniform. God is conceived on all sides as timeless, immutable, omniscient, omnipotent, supremely good, and – what is most remarkable – a person, who praises and blames, loves, hates and forgives, and acts by moral categories. Such a conception is bound to be problematic, since it runs to extremes in every direction, while clinging to the idea that *we* are made in God's image – a sure sign, for the cynic, that he is made in ours. Nevertheless, no other conception will really answer to our need – the need to find a transcendental *subject*, for whom all other subjects are knowable in their subjectivity, and who has the power and the will to heal the fissure in our world.

In the last chapter I discussed the impetus to pass from the temporal to the timeless, while supposing that one and the same entity can survive the change. There is a parallel impetus to pass from the contingent to the necessary, while holding all other things constant. This is illustrated in one of the five arguments for God's existence (the 'Five Ways') with which St Thomas Aquinas begins his great *Summa Theologica*. We find ourselves, Aquinas argues, in a world of contingent things: things which might not have existed. It is possible for such things both to be and not to be. But that which might not be, at some time is not. If everything exists contingently, therefore, there must be a time at which there is nothing. But if that is ever true, nothing would exist thereafter, since nothing comes of nothing. So there would be nothing now. But there *is* something now. Therefore not everything that exists exists contingently. Something exists necessarily. And this thing with 'necessary being' is God.

This 'argument from contingent being' has the same dry and abstract flavour as the ontological argument, with which it is often compared. As stated by St Anselm, the ontological argument runs as follows: we understand by God a being greater than which nothing can be thought. This idea clearly exists in our minds: it is the idea of a being endowed with every positive attribute and every perfection. But if the object of this idea were to exist solely in our mind, and not in reality, there would be an idea of something superior to it, namely of the being that possessed not only all the perfections already conceived, but also the additional perfection of real existence. Which is contrary to hypothesis. Hence the idea of a most perfect being must correspond to reality. Existence belongs to the nature of the most perfect being: it follows from his nature that he exists. In other words, he exists necessarily and not contingently.

Kant responded to this argument by saying that existence is not a predicate: and modern logic agrees with him. (In saying that something with predicates F, G, and H *exists*, you do not add to the list of its properties: you say that F, G, and H are *instantiated* in a single instance.) But nobody has been able to prove that the argument assumes that existence *is* a predicate. In fact nobody has been able to prove very much about the argument at all. Ingenious versions continue to issue from the pens of half-crazed logicians, and while none of them is wholly believable, they serve the useful purpose of showing the rumours of God's death to be greatly exaggerated.

But 'necessary being' lands us again in the timeless realm: indeed, it is the same idea. Timeless beings cannot go out of existence, since they cannot come into existence either. Their existence follows from their concept. And the same is true of God. But how in that case does God relate to the world? Numbers have necessary being – if the number 2 exists at all, then it exists in all possible worlds. But it purchases its necessary existence at the expense of its causal power. Numbers have no ability to act or be acted upon. (Imagine being told one morning that the number 2 had suffered a dreadful calamity during the night.) And the same ought to be true of all things with necessary being: if something *exists* by necessity, then it should have all its properties by necessity too. Maybe there is such a thing, and maybe it has all 'perfections' – or at least, all perfections which are not bound up with the idea of change. But there's the rub. The perfection of a person is linked inextricably with action, emotion, change, and mutability. And God, we are told, is a person.

We could accept the God of the philosophers, therefore, only if we could solve the problem that has already confronted us, of identifying one and the same individual in the timeless and the temporal sphere. The Christian doctrine of incarnation claims to do just that; but that doctrine is the greatest of mysteries, and certainly not a proof. (Consider how Milton has to amend it, in order to make the Christ of *Paradise Lost* intelligible.) We seem to have reached an impasse. God answers to our need, only if he is a person like us. But that possibility seems to be ruled out by his necessary and timeless being. In which case, of what conceivable use could he be?

It was Max Stirner who announced to the world in 1845 that God is dead. Nietzsche, repeating the obituary in *Thus Spake Zarathustra*, was acutely aware that mankind would find it hard to live with the news, and therefore that something should be offered as a consolation. If there is no transcendental being, he suggested, then our aspirations can be met only by *self*-transcendence, by the overcoming of human nature, in that higher and stronger version of it, which is the *Übermensch*. A few disciples tried to follow

Nietzsche's advice, with results as a rule so disagreeable to others, as to discredit the attempt. The least that can be said is that, if you *are* an *Übermensch*, then it is better to keep quiet about it. In fact Nietzsche's morality of self-transcendence shows the meaning of religion for beings like us: faith is a supreme overcoming of our transcendental loneliness; without it, either we make a virtue of that loneliness, as Nietzsche did, or we live at some less exalted level. The announcement of the death of God is less a statement about God, than a statement about us. Even if the abstruse arguments for a 'necessary being' proved to be valid, and even if we could attach to that being some of the features of personality, as these are known to us, this would not revive the religious attitude. For it would not revive the mystic communion of the faithful, through which the face of the world is revealed. The death of God really means the death of an old form of human community – a community founded on holiness.

The concepts of the holy and the sacred are, or ought to be, of considerable interest to the philosopher. For they show how great the disparity can be, between the concepts through which we perceive the world, and those which we use to explain it. In Chapter 1 I considered a familiar example of this disparity: the human smile. Milton tells us that 'Smiles from Reason flow,/ And are of love the food'. He means that only self-conscious, reasoning beings smile, since only they have the peculiar *intentionality* which is expressed in smiling. (Mercifully, Milton didn't express himself in those terms.) Yet smiles would not appear in the scientist's 'book of the world'. All that you would find there is an account of the face and its muscles, and of the response of the face to electro-chemical signals originating in the brain. We classify facial movements as smiles, because that is how we perceive and respond to them, as components in the dialogue of persons. There is an attitude that we direct towards the human person, and which leads us to see in the human form a perspective on the world that reaches from a point outside it. That is what we see in a smile. And the experience of the holy, the sacred and the miraculous arises in a similar way, when we direct this attitude not to other human beings, but to places, times, and objects, so that they are lifted from their mute contingency into the dialogue of reason. A sacred place is one in which personality shines from mere *objects*: from a piece of stone, a tree, or a patch of water. Such things have no subjectivity of their own: which is why they convey the sense of God's presence. The experience of the sacred is therefore a revelation, a direct encounter with the divine, which eludes all explanation in natural terms, and stands isolated and apart.

This ability to see the world in personal terms overcomes human estrangement. It arises from a superfluity of social feeling, when the experience of membership overflows into nature, and fills it with a human animation. It confirms our freedom, by providing the mirror in which freedom can be seen. Nature then ceases to be a prison; its doors stand open, and no shadow falls between the intention and the act.

We have lost that image. The old forms of community have disappeared, and science has laid a stern interdiction over any view of nature but its own. In place of a natural world made in the image of humanity, we find a humanity redescribed, as part of the natural world. The scientific picture of the human being has replaced the theological; indeed, it has demoralized the world, by scrubbing out the mark of human freedom. But the demoralized world is not the real one, and it is the task of philosophy to show that this is so.

8

Freedom

Can this be done? Can philosophy restore the faith in human freedom, when science seems so entirely to dispense with it? I believe that the answer is yes. But there is no greater proof of human freedom, than the vested interest in denying it; and philosophy, which persuades only by speaking softly, is unlikely to win by a show of hands.

We make choices, and carry them out; we praise and blame one another for our acts and omissions; we deliberate about the future and make up our minds. Like the animals, we have desires; but, unlike the animals, we also make choices – we can choose to do what we do not want to do, and want to do what we do not choose. All these facts seem to imply that we are free to do more than one thing, and that what we actually do is our choice, and our responsibility.

The belief in freedom seems at first sight to conflict with scientific determinism, which is the view that every event has a cause, and that every event is also *determined* by its cause. A determines B if B *has* to happen, given A. The usual argument given for determinism is that the relation between cause and effect is 'law-like': one event causes another only if there is a law connecting them. And laws have no exceptions. In which case, given the sum of true scientific laws, and a complete description of the universe at any one time, a complete description of the universe at any other time may be deduced. Hence the way the world is at any future time is fully determined by the way the world is now. This goes for my actions too. What I shall do at any future moment is therefore inexorable, given present (and past) conditions. So how can I be free?

A very old-fashioned view of science is supposed in that account. Scientific laws do have exceptions. They tell us, as a rule, what is probable, given certain conditions. Quantum mechanics holds that even the ultimate laws of the universe must be phrased in terms of probabilities. It is therefore never true that the effect *must* follow, given the cause; only, at best, that it is very likely to follow.

This does not remove the problem, however. For even if the law connecting cause and effect is expressed in terms of probability, it is still the case that the effect was produced by the cause, which was produced by its cause, and so on *ad infinitum*. Hence an action is the result of causes which stretch back in time, to some point before the agent's own existence. His wielding the dagger was caused by movements in the muscles which were caused by impulses in the nerves which were ... Eventually we emerge from the series of causes at the other side of the human person, in a place where he is not. So what part did *he* play in the action, given that the conditions were in place before his birth which were to lead to it? And in what sense was he free to do otherwise?

The problem with such an argument is that it is essentially rhetorical: it is an attempt to shift the burden of proof onto those who believe in freedom. Instead of proving that we are not free, it asks us to prove that we are. But why should we do that, when it is *obvious* that we are free, and when we have yet to be given an argument for thinking otherwise? Hume argued that the idea of freedom arises when we attribute the consequences of an action to the agent, by way of praise and blame. There is nothing in this idea that either affirms or denies determinism, and its grounds are unaffected by the advance of science. Our problem arises because we neglect to ask what we are doing, in describing an action as free. Only if we know what we are doing, will we really understand the concept: and the belief that an action, to be free, must be free from the chain of causes, results either from intellectual indolence, or from a misguided will to believe.

But what exactly *are* we doing, in describing an action as free? The problem of free-will is easily run together with another – the problem of the subject, and its relation to the world of objects. In a magnificent work of synthesis, Kant argued that only a 'transcendental subject' *could* be free, that such a subject is essentially outside nature, and that its freedom is also a form of obedience – obedience not to causal laws, but to the necessary and eternal laws of reason. He then had the task of showing how this transcendental subject could act *in* the realm of nature, and manifest its freedom here and now. In other words, he stumbled across another 'point of intersection of the timeless with time'. In the end, he was inclined to say, we *know* that we are free, since freedom is the pre-condition of all decision-making, including the decision to worry about freedom; at the same time we cannot understand this thing that we know, since the understanding stops at the threshold of the transcendental. Whatever lies beyond the threshold cannot be brought under concepts, and therefore cannot be thought. To which there is an obvious response: have you not brought it under concepts, in explaining the problem? If not, perhaps you should heed the last proposition of Wittgenstein's *Tractatus* – 'That whereof we cannot speak, we must consign to silence'.

Like all attempts to say what cannot be said, Kant's takes up many pages. Its point is revealed, not in the unsayable conclusions, but in the intelligible approach to them. The first step in that approach is to put aside the word 'freedom', and look instead at the practice in which it occurs: the practice of holding people to account for what they do. Imagine walking down a street, minding your own business, when suddenly confronted by a mugger. Without regard for your desires or feelings in the matter, he strikes you to the ground, removes your wallet, and walks calmly away as you nurse your wounds. If there is such a thing as a free action, then this was it. Not only do you condemn the mugger; you and others will seek to punish him, and feel anger and resentment so long as he goes free. He is responsible for your loss, for your wounds, and for your damaged peace of mind: he acted deliberately in causing your suffering, and cared for nothing but his own advantage.

Imagine a slightly different case. You have entrusted your child to your friend for the day, being called away on urgent business, and the child being too young to look after itself. Your friend, intending no harm, but drinking more than he should, leaves the child to its own devices, with the result that it strays into the road and is injured by a passing car. Nobody in this situation acted deliberately so as to cause the child's injury. But your friend was nevertheless responsible. His negligence was the key factor in the catastrophe, since by neglecting his duty, he made the accident more likely. To say that he neglected his duty is to say that there are things which he ought to have done which he left undone. You are angry and resentful; you reproach him; and lay the blame for the accident at his door.

Imagine yet another case. You have asked someone to look after your child, and he does so scrupulously, until suddenly called away by a cry of distress from the house next door. While he is absent, helping his neighbour, who would have died without his assistance, your child wanders into the roadway and is injured. You hold your friend responsible at first, are angry and reproachful; but on learning all the facts, you acknowledge that he acted rightly, in the circumstances, and is therefore not to blame.

The three cases illustrate the idea, fundamental to all human relations, of responsibility. They show that a person can be held to account, not only for what he does deliberately, but also for the consequences of what he does not do. And they show that responsibility is mitigated by excuses, and enhanced by negligence or self-centred disregard. If you study the law of negligence, or the legal concept of 'diminished responsibility', you will see that the absolute distinction that we may be tempted to draw, between free and unfree actions, is no more than a philosophical gloss on a distinction which is not absolute at all, but a distinction of degree. Persons are the subject of a constant moral accounting, and our attitudes towards them are shaped by this. This is the heart of the social practice which gives the concept of freedom its sense.

Let us look first at ordinary personal relations: relations of familiarity, friendship and co-operation, on which our daily lives depend. If someone deliberately injures another, or negligently causes injury, the victim will feel resentment, and perhaps a desire for retribution or revenge. The first step in normal relations, however, is to reproach the person who has wronged you. He may then recognize his fault, and ask to be forgiven. Perhaps he shows a willingness to atone for it, through deliberately depriving himself for your benefit. And perhaps, at the end of this process, you are prepared to forgive him and, having done so, discover that your original feelings towards him are restored. This process is familiar to us in many guises: wrongdoing, reproach, confession, atonement and forgiveness form the stages away from and back to equilibrium in relations of friendship, co-operation and love. The Christian religion recognizes these stages as fundamental, too, in our relation to God. Only if the wrongdoer refuses to recognize his fault, do the original feelings of resentment and desire for revenge continue. For now the wrongdoer is setting aside the norms of peaceful conduct, and throwing down a challenge.

To take up this challenge is to act in the name not of friendship, but of justice. Where friendship desires reconciliation, and therefore atonement, justice demands retribution, and therefore punishment: one and the same process may be viewed as either – but what makes it atonement or punishment is the intention with which it is inflicted or assumed.

Both these processes show a search for equilibrium. And both are possible only between persons, whose actions are shaped and opposed through reasoned dialogue. It is always true that I could relate to other persons as I do to objects, studying the laws of motion that govern them, and adjusting their behaviour through the application of medical and biological science. But this would be to step outside the moral dialogue, to treat the other as a *mere* object, and to circumvent the normal paths to equilibrium. When human beings treat others in this way, it strikes us as sinister, uncanny, even devilish. On the other hand, with certain people, moral dialogue is useless: it makes no difference to them that they inspire resentment, anger or outrage. However we treat them, they will never mend their ways – either because they do not understand the need for this, or because they are driven by impulses which they cannot control. In such cases we begin to renounce the moral dialogue; we feel entitled to treat the other as an object; entitled to apply to him our store of scientific knowledge; entitled to bypass his consent, when seeking a remedy for his bad behaviour.

The point has been made in other terms by the Oxford philosopher, Sir Peter Strawson, who argues that reactions like resentment and anger are reasonable in part because they are *effective*. In normal cases, we have a far more effective way of influencing people's behaviour, by responding to them in this way, than is made available by any 'objective' science. Strawson suggests that the conflict between freedom and causality is not a conflict *in rem*, but a conflict between two kinds of attitude: the interpersonal and the scientific. Interpersonal emotion gives us a far more effective handle on the world than we could ever obtain through a science of human behaviour. But there comes a point where the interpersonal approach ceases to bring rewards. It is then that we begin to look for causes; it is then that we demote the other from person to thing – or, to revert to the Kantian language, from subject to object.

Now let us return to the idea of freedom. You can see at once that we don't actually *need* this word. We can say what we want to say in terms of the more flexible notions of responsibility, accountability, and excuses. These are the ideas that we employ, in order to describe people as partners in the moral dialogue. They take their sense from the practices of giving and taking *reasons for action*, of ascribing rights and obligations, of assessing people in the constant and ongoing dialogue which is the norm of human society.

We can now move a little further down the path towards the unsayable thing that Kant sought to say. When we 'hold someone responsible' for a state of affairs, we do not necessarily imply that his actions caused it. Nor do we hold someone responsible for everything that he deliberately does. (Excuses may erase responsibility.) The judgement of responsibility attaches an event, not to the actions of a person, but to the person himself. We are, so to speak, summoning him to judgement. And if we use the word 'cause' in such a case, it is usually in a special way – to say, not that your *actions* were the cause, but that *you* were the cause. In other words, the term 'cause' no longer links two events, but links an *event* to a *person*, so as to *charge* him with it.

But how is this link established? Causation seems to be neither necessary, nor sufficient. Nor does the link exist only between a person and the present or past. You can take responsibility for the future, and this 'assumption' of responsibility entitles others to praise or blame you in the light of what transpires. Relations of responsibility, unlike causal relations, are also negotiable. We may, as a result of reasoned dialogue, reduce or increase your 'accountability' for an accident. The relation of the person to the event is not established at the time of the event, nor at any time in particular, but only when the case is 'brought to judgement'. Judgements of responsibility are just that – judgements, making appeal to the impartial court of reason, in which we are equal suitors for our rights. Already we may be tempted to say that the judgement of responsibility does not link objects to objects, but objects to subjects, who stand judged by their fellow subjects in another sphere.

I remarked on the fact that our attitudes to people may shift from the interpersonal to the scientific, when the first prove unrewarding. The same shift may occur in our attitude to ourselves. Consider the following dialogue:

A: What are you going to do, now that your wife has left?

B: I shall take up mountaineering.

A: Why?

B: Because it is good, when life has lost its zest, to put yourself in danger.

B has expressed a decision, and found reasons to justify it. His sincerity is proved hereafter by what he does. If he makes no effort to take up this dangerous occupation, then doubt is cast on whether he meant what he said.

Suppose, however, that the dialogue proceeds as follows:

A: What are you going to do, now that your wife has left?

B: I expect I shall take to drink.
A: Why?
B: I seem to be made that way.

Here B has expressed no decision, but only a prediction. And he supports his prediction not with a justifying reason, but with evidence – i.e., with a reason for believing, rather than a reason for doing, something. Clearly B's attitude towards his future, in this second example, is very different from the attitude expressed in the first. He is now looking on it from outside, as though it were the future of someone else, and as though he had no part in it. In making a decision I project myself into the future, make myself accountable for it, and look on it as part of *myself*. Furthermore, if you ask how B *knows* that he will take up mountaineering, when he has decided to do so, there is no answer other than 'he has decided to do so'. His knowledge is based on nothing, since it is an immediate expression of his conscious self. If you ask, in the second case, how he knows that he will take to drink, then the answer is to be found in the evidence he uses. In the case of a prediction, he can make a mistake. In the case of a decision there is no room for mistakes, and non-performance must be explained in another way – either as insincerity, or a change of mind.

This distinction touches on the very essence of rational agency. The person who only predicts the future, but never decides, has fallen out of dialogue with others. He is drifting in the world like an object, and sees himself in just that way. Only the person who decides can take a part in moral dialogue, and only he can relate to others as persons do – not drifting beside them, but engaging with them in his feelings, as one self-conscious being engages with another. And surely, there is nothing forced in the suggestion that the person who only predicts his behaviour sees himself as an object, whereas he who decides is seeing himself as a subject.

We are closer still to the unsayable thing that Kant wanted to say: to the idea that I am both an object in nature, and a subject outside it, and that freedom is lost when the subject surrenders to the object.

And perhaps we can stop here, without stepping over the threshold. Perhaps it is enough to say that we can see ourselves and others in two different ways: as parts of nature, obedient to the laws of causality, or as self-conscious agents, who take responsibility for the world in which they act. But these two 'aspects' are so very different, that there will always be a problem as to how they are related, and the problem will not be less intractable than that of the relation between the timeless and time. Moreover, we can now see just what is at stake in the confrontation between science and philosophy, and how there is indeed a 'consolation of philosophy', even in the disenchanted world we live in. By philosophizing we have lifted human action out of the web of causal reasoning in which it is ensnared by science. We have discovered concepts which are indispensable to our lives as rational beings, yet which have no place at all in the scientific view of the world: concepts like person, responsibility, freedom and the subject, which shape the world in readiness for action, and which describe the way in which we appear to one another, regardless of what, from the point of view of science, we are.

It is with such concepts that the human world is formed. Our attitudes depend upon the way in which we conceptualize each other. You can feel resentment towards another only if you see him as responsible for what he does, and this means applying to him the concepts that I have been discussing in this chapter. Interpersonal attitudes like love, liking, admiration, disapproval and contempt, all depend upon this system of concepts, and to the extent that those attitudes are indispensable to us, and the foundation of happiness in this or any world, then these concepts cannot be replaced. Of course, I can adopt the scientific approach to human beings as to anything else: and, as I argued in the first chapter, it is in the nature of science to sweep away appearances in favour of the underlying reality which explains them. The explanation of the facts on which our interpersonal attitudes are based would describe a world very different from the world of appearances, and one that could no longer be conceptualized in the way that we require. If the fundamental facts about John are, for me, his biological constitution, his scientific essence, his neurological organization, then I shall find it difficult to respond to him with affection, anger, love, contempt or grief. So described, he becomes mysterious to me, since those classifications do not capture the 'intentional object' of my interpersonal attitudes: the person *as he is conceived*.

In the last chapter I described the concept of the sacred, and the feelings which depend on it. The sense of the sacred, I suggested, derives from the fact that the meaning which we find in the human person can be found also in objects — in places, times and artefacts, in a shrine, a gathering, a place of pilgrimage or prayer. This 'encounter with the subject' in a world of objects is our 'homecoming'; it is the overcoming of the metaphysical isolation which is the lot of rational beings everywhere. Nothing in the scientific view of things forbids the experience of the sacred: science tells us only that this experience, like every other, has a natural and not a supernatural cause. Those who seek for meanings may be indifferent to causes, and those who communicate with God through prayer should be no more cut off from him by the knowledge that the world of objects does not contain him, than they are cut off from those they love by the knowledge that words, smiles and gestures are nothing but movements of the flesh. But the scientific worldview contains a fatal temptation: it invites us to regard the subject as a myth, and to see the world under one aspect alone, as a world of objects. And this disenchanted world is also a world of alienation.

We should not forget that the attempt to re-create the human world through science has already been made. Marx's theory of history, and the Nazi science of race are very bad examples of science. But they licensed forms of government in which the scientific view of our condition was for the first time in power. People were seen as objects, obedient to natural laws; and their happiness was to be secured by experts, acting as the theory prescribed. The theory informed the believer that God is dead, and that with him has been extinguished the divine spark in man. Human freedom is nothing but an appearance on the face of nature; beneath it rides the same implacable causality, the same sovereign indifference, which prepares death equally and unconcernedly for all of us, and which tells us that beyond death there is nothing. The sense of the sacred warns us that there are things which cannot be touched, since to meddle with them is to open a door in the world of objects, so as to stand in the I of God. The desacralized view of the world annihilates that sense, and therefore removes the most important of our prohibitions. In describing the Nazi death-camps Hannah Arendt wrote (*Eichmann in Jerusalem*) of a 'banalization' of evil. It would be better to speak of a 'de-personalization', a severance of evil from the network of personal responsibility. The totalitarian system, and the extermination camp which is its most sublime expression, embody the conviction that nothing is sacred. In such a system, human life is driven underground, and the ideas of freedom and responsibility – ideas without which our picture of man as a moral subject disintegrates entirely – have no public recognition, and no place in the administrative process. If it is so easy to destroy people in such a system, it is because human life enters the public world already destroyed, appearing only as an object among others, to be dealt with by experts versed in the science of man.

Even if we did not have before us the reality of the Nazi and Communist experiments, we have those works of fiction by Orwell, Huxley and Koestler, which warn us what the world must inevitably become, when humanity is surrendered to science. To see human beings as objects is not to see them as they are, but to change what they are, by erasing the appearance through which they relate to one another as persons. It is to create a new kind of creature, a depersonalized human being, in which subject and object drift apart, the first into a world of helpless dreams, the second to destruction. In a very real sense, therefore, there cannot be a science of man: there cannot be a science which explores what we are for one another, when we respond to each other as persons. In what follows we will see in more detail why that is so.

9

Morality

People are bound by moral laws, which articulate the idea of a community of rational beings, living in mutual respect, and resolving their disputes by negotiation and agreement.

Kant tells us that we are to act 'on that maxim which we can will as a law for all rational beings'; we are to treat rational beings as ends, and never as means only; we are to act with a view to the 'kingdom of ends' in which all rational goals are reconciled. These highly abstract principles (which Kant calls 'formal') are less significant than the procedure which is implied in them. Persons have a unique and precious means to resolve their conflicts – a means denied to the rest of nature. For they are able to recognize each other as free beings, who take responsibility for their decisions, and who possess rights against, and duties towards, their kind. The ideas of freedom, responsibility, right and duty contain a tacit assumption that every player in the moral game counts for one, and no player for more than one. By thinking in these terms we acknowledge each person as an irreplaceable and self-sufficient member of the moral order. His rights, duties and responsibilities are his own personal possessions. Only he can renounce or fulfil them, and only he can be held to account should his duties go unfulfilled. If this were not so, the 'moral law', as Kant calls it, would cease to fulfil its purpose, of reconciling individuals in a society of strangers.

As Kant himself pointed out, the moral law has an absolute character. Rights cannot be arbitrarily overridden, or weighed against the profit of ignoring them. Duties cannot be arbitrarily set aside, or cancelled by the bad results of due obedience. I must respect your right, regardless of conflicting interests, since you alone can renounce or cancel it. That is the point of the concept – to provide an absolute barrier against invasion. A right is an interest that is given special protection, and which cannot be overridden or cancelled without the consent of the person who possesses it. By describing an interest as a right we lift it from the account of cost and benefit, and place it in the sacred precinct of the self.

Likewise duty, if it is to exist at all, must have an absolute character. A duty can be set aside only when it ceases to be a duty – only when it has been fulfilled or cancelled. There can be conflicts of rights and conflicts of duties: but these conflicts are painful precisely because they cannot be resolved. We weigh rights against each other, and give precedence to the one which we believe to be more serious – as when we take food that belongs to John in order to save the life of the starving Henry. Henry's right to help takes precedence over John's right to his property; nevertheless John's right remains, and John is wronged by the act which succours Henry. The issues here are deep and complex. Suffice it to say that any attempt to deprive the concepts of right and duty of this absolute character would also deprive them of their utility. We should thereby rid ourself of the supreme instrument which reason provides, whereby to live with others while respecting their freedom, their individuality and their sovereignty over the life that is theirs. That is what it means, in the last analysis, to treat a person as an end in himself: namely, to acknowledge his rights against us, and our duties towards him, and to recognize that neither right nor duty can be cancelled by some other good. To put the moral law in a nutshell, it tells us that people must be treated as subjects, not as objects; and this means that rights must be respected, and duties fulfilled.

But the prominence of the moral law in our daily negotiations should not lead us to suppose that morality is merely a system of rules. The moral community is shaped by negotiation, but depends upon many other factors for its life and vitality. In particular it depends upon the affections of those who compose it, and upon their ability to make spontaneous and self-sacrificing gestures for the good of others. A society ordered entirely by the moral law, in which rights, duties and justice take precedence over all interests and affections, would alienate the mere human beings who compose it, and soon fall apart. For it would make no distinction between neighbours and strangers, between the alien and the friend. People need the safety promised by the moral law, and by the habit of negotiation. But they also need something more: the nexus of affection and sympathy which binds them to their neighbours, which creates a common destiny, and which leads people to share one another's sorrows and joys.

While we esteem the punctilious person who performs all his duties, claims no more than he has a right to, and meticulously respects the rights of others, we cannot really love him, unless he is moved by affection too. But affection requires us to bend the rules, to set aside our rights in the interest of those we love, to do that which is beyond the call of duty, and sometimes to dispense our favours unjustly. And the same is true of sympathy – that generalized affection which spreads from the self in dwindling ripples across the world of others. Actions which spring from sympathy may resemble those commanded by the moral law; but they spring from another motive, and one that is just as necessary to the moral life. The moral being is not merely the rule-governed person who plays the game of rights and duties; he has a distinctive emotional character, which both fits him for the moral life and extends and modifies its edicts. He is a creature of extended sympathies, motivated by love, admiration, shame and a host of other social emotions.

Hence we judge moral beings not only in terms of their actions, but also in terms of their motives and characters. For we recognize that the moral law is not a sufficient motive; we obey its precepts only when sufficiently prompted by our character and feelings. Guilt, remorse and shame arrest our weaknesses, just as praise, admiration and approval reinforce our obedience. We depend on these social emotions, since it is the web of sympathy that fortifies our moral resolve. We may not consciously acknowledge it, but we nevertheless know that social order is a precarious thing, which cannot be sustained by law alone. Internal and external threats to it can be deterred only if people have the mettle to resist them – the force of character, the emotional equilibrium and the live human sympathies that will prompt them to persist in a cause, to make sacrifices, and to commit themselves to others. This is the origin of the vital distinction that we make, between vice and virtue. In addition to the moral law, therefore, morality involves the pursuit of virtue, and the avoidance of vice.

The virtues that inspire our admiration are also the qualities which preserve society, whether from external threat or from internal decay: courage and resolution in the face of danger; loyalty and decency in private life; justice and charity in the public sphere. At different periods and in different conditions the emphasis shifts – virtue is malleable, and shaped by material, spiritual and religious circumstances. Nevertheless, the constancy of the objects of human admiration is more significant than the local variations. The antique virtues of courage, prudence, wisdom, temperance and justice, amplified by Christian charity and pagan loyalty, still form the core idea of human excellence. It is these qualities that we admire, that we wish for in those we love, and hope to be credited with ourselves.

Such qualities require a social setting. They are not solipsistic achievements like the muscles of the body-builder, or the mortification of the anchorite. Only in the context of human admiration and contempt does the virtuous character emerge, and only in the condition of society is virtue properly exercised and rightly understood. But this social setting is also an emotional setting, and emotions are reactions not to the world as it is in itself, but to the world as it is understood. The world is understood differently by people and animals. Our world, unlike theirs, contains rights, obligations and duties; it is a world of self-conscious subjects, in which events are divided into the free and the unfree, those which have reasons, and those which are merely caused, those which stem from a rational subject, and those which erupt in the stream of objects with no conscious design. Thinking of the world in this way, we respond to it with emotions that lie beyond the repertoire of other animals: indignation, resentment and envy; admiration, commitment and erotic love – all of which involve the thought of the other as a free subject, with rights and duties and a self-conscious vision of his past and future. Only moral beings can feel these emotions, and in feeling them they situate themselves in some way outside the natural order, standing back from it in judgement.

The sympathies of moral beings are also marked by this detachment from the natural order. A horse will run when the herd runs; a hound excited by a scent will communicate his excitement to his fellows; a partridge will throw herself between her brood and the fox that threatens them. The casual observer might see these actions as expressing sympathy – as animated by a feeling which in some way takes account of the feelings and interests of others. But they lack a crucial ingredient, which is the *thought of what the other is feeling*. In none of the cases that I have mentioned (and they form three archetypes of animal 'sympathy') do we need to invoke this very special thought in order to explain the animal's behaviour. It is a thought which is peculiar to moral beings, involving a recognition of the distinction between self and other, and of the other as *feeling what I might have felt*. Even the dog who is distressed by his master's sickness lacks this thought. His emotion is not compassion, but anxiety, as the source of his borrowed life runs thin.

Two of our sympathetic feelings are of great moral importance: pity towards those who suffer, and pleasure in another's joy. Both feelings are held to be part of human virtue. Pitiless people and joyless people alike awaken our disapproval. True, Nietzsche mounted an assault on pity, and on the 'herd morality' which he supposed to be contained in it. But most people remain unpersuaded, and rightly so. For pity and good cheer are complementary. You cannot rejoice in the joys of others, without suffering their pains, and all pleasure requires the sympathy of others if it is to translate itself into joy. It seems to me, indeed, that there is something deeply contradictory in a philosophy that advocates joyful wisdom, while slandering pity as the enemy of the higher life.

Indeed, whether we look at these emotions from the point of view of the individual, or from that of society, we cannot fail to see them as indispensable parts of human goodness. Sympathy awakens sympathy: it draws us to itself, and forms the bond of goodwill from which our social affections grow. Pitiless and joyless people are also affectionless; if they love, it is with a hard, dogged love that threatens to destroy what it cherishes. We avoid them as unnatural, and also dangerous. The anger of a pitiless person is to be feared; as is the friendship of a joyless one. It is not the pitiless and the joyless who sustain the social order: on the contrary, they are parasites, who depend on the overspill of sympathy which misleads us into forgiving them. Nietzsche condemned pity for favouring the weak and the degenerate. In fact, pity is a necessary part of any society which is able to heal itself, and to overcome disaster. It is indispensable in war as in peace, since it causes people to stand side by side with strangers in their shared misfortune, and arouses them to anger and revenge against the common enemy.

There is another component in our moral thinking, in addition to the moral law, and the sympathy which extends the scope of it – the component which I shall call, borrowing from Roman usage, piety, meaning the respect for sacred things. *Pietas* requires that we honour our parents and ancestors, the household deities, the laws and the civil order, that we keep the appointed festivals and public ceremonies – and all this out of a sense of the sacred given-ness of these things, which are not our invention, and to which we owe an unfathomable debt of gratitude. It seems to me that, beneath all moral sentiment, there lies a deep layer of pious feeling. It is a feeling which does not depend explicitly on religious belief, and which no moral being can really escape, however little he may overtly acknowledge it. Utilitarians may regard pious feelings as the mere residue of moral thinking; but, as the argument of the last two chapters implies, they are not a residue at all. Put in simple terms, piety means the deep down recognition of our frailty and dependence, the acknowledgement that the burden we inherit cannot be sustained unaided, the disposition to give thanks for our existence and reverence to the world on which we depend, and the sense of the unfathomable mystery which surrounds our coming to be and our passing away. All these feelings come together in our humility before the works of nature, and this humility is the fertile soil in which the seeds of morality are planted. The three forms of moral life that I have described – respect for persons, the pursuit of virtue and natural sympathy – all depend, in the last analysis, on piety. For piety instils the readiness to be guided and instructed, and the knowledge of our own little-ness which make the gift of moral conduct – whereby we are lifted from our solitude – so obviously desirable.

Piety is rational, in the sense that we all have reason to feel it. It is also a vital asset of society, since it forestalls the desecration of established things. Nevertheless, piety is not, in any clear sense, *amenable to reason*. Indeed, it marks out another place where reasoning comes to an end. The same is true, it seems to me, of many moral attitudes and feelings: while it is supremely rational to possess them, they are not themselves amenable to reason, and the attempt to make them so produces the kind of ludicrous caricature of morality that we witness in utilitarianism.

This does not mean that we must simply accept one another's prejudices. On the contrary, morality fails of its purpose, if people cannot reach agreement, and amend their views and feelings in the light of experience, with a view to accommodating others. It means, rather, that we should not expect a 'decision procedure' which will settle moral ques-tions finally and unambiguously. In these areas the task of reason is to clarify our intuitions, to recognize the nature and extent of our commitments, and to search for the points of agreement which will provide a fulcrum on which our prejudices may be turned.

It may be that, if we knew all the facts, the natural operation of sympathy would lead us to agree in our judge-ments: so thought Hume. But the historical character of our passions and pieties means that they come into existence fatally entangled in the circumstances that produced them, and can be converted into universal laws only by severing them from their roots, and draining them of vital force.

It is nevertheless true that, since the Enlightenment, moral thought has shied away from piety and invested its greatest energy in those abstract legal ideas associated with the respect for persons. This has happened for many reasons, and it is not my purpose to examine them. But it is not unreasonable to believe that spoliation, over-production and the destruction of the environment all spring from a single source, which is the loss of piety. However deep it may be concealed within our psyche, piety is by no means a redundant part of the moral consciousness but, on the contrary, the source of our most valuable social emotions. It is piety, and not reason, that implants in us the respect for the world, for its past and its future, and which impedes us from pillaging all we can before the light of consciousness fails in us.

It is piety, too, which causes us to exalt the human form in life and art. Perhaps there are moral beings who are not humans: angels, devils and divinities, if they exist. But we have no direct experience of them. We have no clear *image* of morality save the image of the human form; such doubts as we feel about the elephant, the dolphin and the chimpanzee are too insecure to revise the overwhelming authority, for us, of the human face and gesture:

> For Mercy has a human heart,
> Pity a human face,
> And Love the human form divine,
> And Peace, the human dress.

Blake's words flow from the fount of reverence that springs in all of us, and which causes us not merely to cherish the works of unblemished nature, but to look on the human being as somehow exalted above them. I do not mean that all humans are admirable or lovable: far from it. But they are all in some way untouchable. An air of sacred prohibition surrounds humanity, since the 'human form divine' is our only image of the subject – the being who stands above the world of objects, in an attitude of judgement.

It follows from what I have said that there will be four separate sources of moral argument: personality, with its associated moral law; the ethic of virtue; sympathy; and finally piety. Most of our moral difficulties and 'hard cases' derive from the areas where these four kinds of thinking deliver conflicting results.

We do not need to accept Kant's sublime derivation of the categorical imperative, in order to recognize that human beings tend spontaneously to agree concerning the morality of interpersonal relations. As soon as we set our own interests aside, and look on human relations with the eye of the impartial judge, we find ourselves agreeing over the rights and wrongs in any conflict. Whatever their philosophical basis, the following principles of practical reasoning are accepted by all reasonable people:

1. Considerations which justify or impugn one person will, in identical circumstances, justify or impugn another. (The principle of moral equality.)

2. Rights are to be respected.

3. Obligations are to be fulfilled.

4. Agreements are to be honoured.

5. Disputes are to be settled by rational argument and not by force.

6. Persons who do not respect the rights of others, forfeit rights of their own.

Long before Kant's categorical imperative philosophers wrote of such principles as defining the 'natural law' – the law which lies above all actual legal systems, and provides the test of their validity. Some of the principles have been explicitly incorporated into international law – notably the fourth (*pacta sunt servanda*). They provide us with the calculus of rights and duties with which our day to day relations with strangers must be conducted, if we are to live by negotiation and not by force or fraud.

We should see the above principles as 'procedural' (or

'formal', to use Kant's idiom), rather than 'substantive'. They do not tell us what our rights and duties are, but only what it means, to describe an interest as a right, and a decision as a duty. Nevertheless, once this procedure is in place – once human beings are in the habit of settling their disputes by an assignment of rights, responsibilities and duties – it cannot be an open question what our rights and duties are. We will be constrained to settle questions in a manner on which all can agree, and – just as in the common law, which is no more than an extended application of this kind of reasoning – we will tend to agree, just as long as we look on all conflict as though it were the conflict of others, and observe it with the eye of an impartial judge. Why this should be so is a deep question, to which Hume and Kant gave conflicting answers. But that it *is* so is surely evident.

Although rational beings, adopting the standpoint of the impartial judge, will tend to endorse the principles given above, it does not follow that they will act on them when their interests tend in some other direction. But there are settled dispositions of character which will ensure that people overcome the temptations posed by greed, self-interest and fear. It is reasonable to admire and cultivate these dispositions, therefore, which owe their reasonableness to the same considerations as justify the moral law. Only the just person will act on the impartial verdict when his own interests conflict with it; only the courageous person will uphold the moral law when others jeer at it; only the temperate person will place rights and duties above the call of appetite. And so on. In short, the traditional virtues provide a source of moral reasoning which endorses the calculus of rights and duties. Whatever reasons we have for accepting the moral law, are reasons for cultivating the virtues.

To the traditional virtues, which prepare us for membership of a moral community, we must add the wider and more flexible virtues which stem from sympathy. Christian charity (caritas, or fellow-feeling) is pre-eminent among these wider virtues. Philosophically speaking, charity is the disposition to put yourself in another's shoes, and to be motivated on his behalf. It is the disposition to feel pain at his suffering, and joy at his joy.

This too is a reasonable motive, for without it the moral community would be deprived of its most vital source of strength, and the individual of the most important reward attached to membership – the pleasure of giving and receiving in reciprocal concern.

It is here, however, that a potential clash arises, between utilitarian ways of thinking and the calculus of rights. The charitable instinct identifies with joy and suffering wherever it finds them and, faced with the bewildering extent of these emotions, finds itself compelled to reason in a utilitarian way. Charity hopes to maximize joy and minimize suffering in general, just as each person spontaneously acts to maximize joy and minimize suffering in himself. To think in this way, however, is to enter into inevitable conflict with the more sophisticated pattern of reasoning that underpins the moral community. I cannot treat persons as the subject-matter of a utilitarian calculation. I cannot inflict deliberate pain on John in order to relieve the twofold suffering of Elizabeth and Mary, without consulting the rights and duties of the parties. We ascribe rights to people precisely because their freedom and their membership of the moral community forbid us from invading their space.

In short, even if utilitarian reasoning is a natural expression of the sympathy on which the moral life depends, reason demands that it be applied only selectively and within the framework established by the moral law. Questions of right, duty and responsibility must be settled first; only then does the utilitarian calculus apply. A few examples will make this clear. Suppose John is suffering from kidney failure, and only one other person, Henry, is of the same blood-group.

With one of Henry's kidneys, John could lead a healthy and normal life, while Henry's life would not be significantly impaired. This utilitarian calculation is entirely irrelevant, when faced with the question whether we ought to compel Henry to release one of his kidneys. For that is something we have no right to do, and all reasoning stops once this moral truth is recognized.

Suppose Elizabeth and Jane are both suffering from a rare disease, and William, Jane's husband, has obtained at great expense a quantity of the only drug that will cure it. By administering the whole quantity to Jane he ensures a 90 per cent chance of her survival; by dividing it between Jane and Elizabeth, he will provide a 60 per cent chance of recovery to both. Again, the utilitarian calculation, which might seem to favour division, is irrelevant. For William has a special responsibility towards his wife, which must be discharged before the welfare of any stranger can be taken into account.

Suppose that Alfred is driving a lorry, for the maintenance of which he is not responsible, and discovers that the brakes have failed. If he swerves to the right he kills a man at a bus-stop; if he takes no action he will run down two pedestrians at a crossing, while if he swerves to the left he will drive into a crowd of children. Here, surely, the utilitarian calculus applies, and Alfred would be blamed for *not* applying it. By swerving to the right he absolves himself of all responsibility for the death of the victim, while at the same time minimizing the human cost of the disaster. The brake-failure is not an action of Alfred's, but a misfortune that afflicts him. His principal duty, in such a case, is to minimize the suffering that results from it.

Such examples show the true goal of utilitarian thinking, which is not to replace or compete with the moral law, but to guide us when the moral law is silent, and when only sympathy speaks. Hence utilitarian reasoning is of the first importance in our dealings with animals – in particular with those animals to which we have no special duty of care. We should not imagine, however, that the utilitarian calculus could ever achieve the mathematical precision which Bentham and his followers have wished for. There is no formula for measuring the value of a life, the seriousness of a creature's suffering, or the extent of its happiness or joy. To reason in a utilitarian way is to reason as Alfred does in my example: through numbers when these are suggested (as here, where Alfred must count the numbers of threatened lives); but otherwise through an assessment of the moral *Gestalt*, asking whether 'things in general would be better if ...'. Those who wish to reduce such reasoning to an econometric calculation rid the moral question of its distinctive character, and replace it with questions of another kind – questions concerning 'preference orderings', 'optimizing' and 'satisficing' solutions, and rational choice under conditions of risk and uncertainty. By shaping the moral question so that it can be fed into the machinery of economics, we do not solve it. On the contrary, we put a fantasy problem for experts in place of the painful reality of moral choice. If the answer to moral questions were really to be found in decision theory, then most people would be unable to discover it. In which case morality would lose its function as a guide to life, offered to all of us by the fact of reasoned dialogue.

Finally, there is the sphere of piety. As I have argued, piety is rational, but not amenable to reason. The person who tries completely to rationalize his pieties has in a sense already lost them. The best we can hope for is a version of what Rawls has called 'reflective equilibrium', in which our pieties are brought into relation with our more critical opinions and modified accordingly, while in their turn influencing our reasoned judgements.

The motive of morality is complex. Were we immortal beings, outside nature and freed from its imperatives, the moral law would be sufficient motive. But we are mortal, passionate creatures, and morality exists for us only because our sympathies endorse it. We are motivated by fellow-feeling, by love of virtue and hatred of vice, by a sense of helplessness and dependence which finds relief in piety, and by a host of socially engendered feelings which have no place in the serene dispensations of a 'Holy Will'. Hence conflicts and dilemmas arise. The attraction of utilitarianism lies in the promise to resolve all these conflicts, by construing moral judgement as a kind of economic calculus. But the promise is illusory, and the effect of believing it repulsive. So how are moral conflicts resolved? How, in particular, should we respond to the situation in which the moral law points in one direction, and sympathy another, or in which the ethic of virtue clashes with the ethic of piety – as it famously did for Agamemnon?

First, let it be said that the moral law, when it speaks, takes precedence. For the moral law can exist on no other terms. Only if a right guarantees its subject-matter does it offer protection to the one who possesses it. Only then do rights perform their role, of defining the position from which moral dialogue begins. The essential function of morality, in creating a community founded in negotiation and consent, requires that rights and duties cannot be sacrificed to other interests.

But rights and duties can conflict. The result is a dilemma, and the distinguishing mark of a dilemma is that, while only one of two things can be done, you have a duty to do both. This duty is not cancelled by the dilemma: you merely have an excuse for not fulfilling it.

When the claims of right and duty have been satisfied, in so far as possible, the claims of virtue must be addressed. Even if the moral law neither forbids nor permits an action, there is still the question whether a virtuous person would perform it. For example, if we thought, as do many of those who defend abortion, that the human foetus has no rights, and that we have no specific duties towards it, we should still not be entitled to conclude that the foetus can be treated in any way we choose. It may nevertheless be the case – and manifestly *is* the case – that certain ways of treating a foetus are vicious, and that there are only some ways of treating it that a good person would contemplate, even when persuaded that a foetus lies outside the protection of the moral law.

Finally, when all requirements of right and virtue have been met, we can respond to the call of sympathy: and here a kind of utilitarian thinking comes into play, as the means to extend our sympathies to all whose interests are affected by our acts. Even so, the authority of this reasoning is not absolute: for sympathy may compete with piety. We rationalize our pieties by measuring them against our sympathies, and discipline our sympathies by testing them against the intuitions which stem from piety.

While this ordering of the four sources of moral reasoning may be questioned, and while it leaves much unresolved, it corresponds, I believe, to the practice of the ordinary conscience, and accords with the underlying purpose of morality. The real problem that confronts us is not that of justifying moral judgements, but that of justifying the concepts on which they depend. It is the problem that is or ought to be the central problem of modern philosophy: how to make sense of the human world?

Sex

Sex is the sphere in which the animal and the personal meet, and where the clash between the scientific and the personal view of things is felt most keenly. It therefore provides the test of any serious moral philosophy, and of any viable theory of the human world.

Until the late nineteenth century it was almost impossible to discuss sex, except as part of erotic love, and even then convention required that the peculiarities of sexual desire remain unmentioned. When the interdiction was finally lifted – by such writers as Krafft-Ebing and Havelock Ellis – it was through offering a 'scientific' approach to a widespread natural phenomenon. Such was the prestige of science that any investigation conducted in its name could call on powerful currents of social approval, which were sufficient to overcome the otherwise crippling reluctance to face the realities of sexual experience. As a result, modern discussions of this experience have been conducted in a 'scientized' idiom which, by its very nature, removes sex from the sphere of interpersonal relations, and remodels it as a relation between objects. Freud's shocking revelations, introduced as neutral, 'scientific' truths about the human condition, were phrased in the terms which are now more or less standard. According to Freud, the aim of sexual desire is 'union of the genitals in the act known as copulation, which leads to a release of the sexual tension and a tempo-

rary extinction of the sexual instinct – a satisfaction analo-
gous to the sating of hunger'. This scientistic image of sexual
desire gave rise, in due course, to the Kinsey report, and is
now part of the standard merchandise of disenchantment. It
seems to me that it is entirely false, and could become true
only by so affecting our sexual emotions, as to change them
into emotions of another kind.

What exactly is sexual pleasure? Is it like the pleasure of
eating and drinking? Like that of lying in a hot bath? Like
that of watching your child at play? Clearly it is both like
and unlike all of these. It is unlike the pleasure of eating, in
that its object is not consumed. It is unlike the pleasure of
the bath, in that it involves taking pleasure *in* an activity,
and in the other person who joins you. It is unlike that of
watching your child at play, in involving bodily sensations
and a surrender to physical desire. Sexual pleasure resembles the pleasure of watching something, however, in a
crucial respect: it has intentionality. It is not just a tingling
sensation; it is a response to another person, and to the act
in which you are engaged with him or her. The other person
may be imaginary: but it is towards a person that your
thoughts are directed, and pleasure depends on thought.

This dependency on thought means that sexual pleasure
can be mistaken, and ceases when the mistake is known.
Although I would be a fool not to jump out of the soothing
bath after being told that what I took for water is really acid,
this is not because I have ceased to feel pleasurable sensations in my skin. In the case of sexual pleasure, the discovery
that it is an unwanted hand that touches me at once extin-
guishes my pleasure. The pleasure could not be taken as
confirming the hitherto unacknowledged sexual virtues of
some previously rejected person. A woman who makes love
to the man who has disguised himself as her husband is no
less the victim of rape, and the discovery of her mistake can
lead to suicide. It is not simply that consent obtained by

fraud is not consent; it is that the woman has been violated, in the very act which caused her pleasure.

What makes a pleasure into a sexual pleasure is the context of arousal. And arousal is not the same as tumescence. It is a 'leaning towards' the other, a movement in the direction of the sexual act, which cannot be separated, either from the thoughts on which it is founded, or from the desire to which it leads. Arousal is a response to the thought of the other as a self-conscious agent, who is alert to me, and who is able to have 'designs' on me. This is evident from the caress and the glance of desire. A caress of affection is a gesture of reassurance – an attempt to place in the consciousness of the other an image of one's own tender concern for him. Not so, however, the caress of desire, which *outlines* the body of the recipient; its gentleness is not that of reassurance only, but that of exploration. It aims to fill the surface of the other's body with a consciousness of your interest – interest, not only in the body, but in the person as embodied. This consciousness is the focal point of the other's pleasure. Sartre writes (*Being and Nothingness*) of the caress as 'incarnating' the other: as though, by your action, you bring the soul into the flesh (the subject into the object) and make it palpable.

The caress is given and received with the same awareness as the glance is given and received. They each have an *epistemic* component (a component of anticipation and discovery). It is hardly surprising, given this, that the face should have such supreme and overriding importance in the transactions of sexual desire. On the scientistic view of sex it is hard to explain why this should be so – why the face should have the power to determine whether we will, or will not, be drawn to seek pleasure in another part. But of course, the face is the picture of the other's subjectivity: it shines with the light of self, and it is as an embodied subject that the other is wanted. Perversion and obscenity involve the eclipse of the subject, as the body and its mechanism are placed in frontal view. In obscenity flesh becomes opaque to the self which lives in it: that is why there is an obscenity of violence as well as an obscenity of sex.

A caress may be either accepted or rejected: in either case, it is because it has been 'read' as conveying a message sent from you to me. I do not receive this message as an explicit act of meaning something, but as a process of mutual discovery, a growing to awareness in you which is also a coming to awareness in me. In the first impulse of arousal, therefore, there is the beginning of that chain of reciprocity which is fundamental to interpersonal attitudes. She conceives her lover conceiving her conceiving him ... not *ad infinitum*, but to the point of mutual recognition of the other, as fully present in his body.

Sexual arousal has, then, an epistemic and interpersonal intentionality. It is a response to another individual, based in revelation and discovery, and involving a reciprocal and co-operative heightening of the common experience of embodiment. It is not directed beyond the other, to the world at large; nor is it transferable to a rival object who might 'do just as well'. Of course, arousal may have its origin in highly generalized thoughts, which flit libidinously from object to object. But when these thoughts have concentrated into the experience of arousal their generality is put aside; it is then the other who counts, and his particular embodiment. Not only the other, but I myself, and the sense of my bodily reality in the other's perspective. Hence arousal, in the normal case, seeks seclusion in a private place, where only the other is relevant to my attention. Indeed, arousal attempts to *abolish* what is not private – in particular to abolish the perspective of the onlooker, of the 'third person' who is neither you nor I.

In Chapter 8 I explored some of the ways in which the subject is realized in the world of objects, and placed great

emphasis on intention, and the distinction between predict-
ing and deciding for the future. But it should not be
supposed that the subject is revealed only through *voluntary*
activity. On the contrary, of equal importance are those
reactions which cannot be willed but only predicted, but
which are nevertheless peculiar to self-conscious beings.
Blushing is a singular instance. Although an involuntary
matter, and – from the physiological point of view – a mere
rushing of blood to the head, blushing is the expression of a
complex thought, and one that places the self on view. My
blush is an involuntary recognition of my accountability
before you for what I am and what I feel. It is an acknowledgement that I stand in the light of your perspective, and
that I cannot hide in my body. A blush is attractive because
it serves both to embody the perspective of the other, and
also at the same time to display that perspective as respon-
sive to me. The same is true of unguarded glances and
smiles, through which the other subject rises to the surface
of his body and makes himself visible. In smiling, blushing,
laughing and crying, it is precisely my loss of control over my
body, and its gain of control over me, that create the immediate experience of an incarnate person. The body ceases at
these moments to be an instrument, and reasserts its natural rights as a person. In such expressions the face does not
function merely as a bodily part, but as the whole person:
the self is spread across its surface, and there 'made flesh'.

The concepts and categories that we use to describe the
embodied person are far removed from the science of the
human body. What place in such a science for smiles as
opposed to grimaces, for blushes as opposed to flushes, for
glances as opposed to looks? In describing your colour as a
blush, I am seeing you as a responsible agent, and situating
you in the realm of embarrassment and self-knowledge. If
we try to describe sexual desire with the categories of human biology, we miss precisely the *intentionality* of sexual

emotion, its directedness towards the embodied subject. The caricature that results describes not desire but perversion. Freud's description of desire is the description of something that we know and shun – or ought to shun. An excitement which concentrates on the sexual organs, whether of man or of woman, which seeks, as it were, to bypass the complex negotiation of the face, hands, voice and posture, is perverted. It voids desire of its intentionality, and replaces it with a pursuit of the sexual commodity, which can always be had for a price.

It is part of the intentionality of desire that a *particular* person is conceived as its object. To someone agitated by his desire for Jane, it is ridiculous to say, 'Take Henrietta, she will do just as well.' Thus there arises the possibility of mistakes of identity. Jacob's desire for Rachel seemed to be satisfied by his night with Leah, only to the extent that, and for as long as, Jacob imagined it was Rachel with whom he was lying. (Genesis 29, v. 22-25; and see the wonderful realization of this little drama in Thomas Mann's *Joseph and his Brothers*.) Our sexual emotions are founded on *individualizing thoughts*: it is *you* whom I want and no other. This individualizing intentionality does not merely stem from the fact that it is persons (in other words, individuals) whom we desire. It stems from the fact that the other is desired as an embodied subject, and not just as a body. You can see the point by drawing a contrast between desire and hunger (a contrast that is expressly negated by Freud). Suppose that people were the only edible things; and suppose that they felt no pain on being eaten and were reconstituted at once. How many formalities and apologies would now be required in the satisfaction of hunger! People would learn to conceal their appetite, and learn not to presume upon the consent of those whom they surveyed with famished glances. It would become a crime to partake of a meal without the meal's consent. Maybe marriage would be the best solution. Still, this predicament is nothing like the predicament in which we are placed by desire. It arises from the lack of anything impersonal to eat, but not from the nature of hunger. Hunger is directed towards the other only as object, and any similar object will serve just as well. It does not individualize the object, or propose any other union than that required by need. When sexual attentions take such a form, they become deeply insulting. And in every form they compromise not only the person who addresses them, but also the person addressed. Precisely because desire proposes a relation between subjects, it forces both parties to account for themselves. Unwanted advances are therefore also forbidden by the one to whom they might be addressed, and any transgression is felt as a contamination. That is why rape is so serious a crime: it is an invasion of the sanctuary which harbours the victim's freedom, and a dragging of the subject into the world of things. If you describe desire in the scientistic terms used by Freud and his followers, the outrage and pollution of rape become impossible to explain. In fact, just about everything in human sexual behaviour becomes impossible to explain – and it is only what might be called the 'charm of disenchantment' that leads people to receive these daft descriptions as the truth.

The intentionality of desire is the topic for a book, and since I have written that book, I shall confine myself here to a few remarks. My hope is to put philosophy to its best use, which is that of shoring up the human world against the corrosive seas of pseudo-science. In true sexual desire, the aim is union with the other, where 'the other' denotes a particular person, with a particular perspective on my actions. The reciprocity which is involved in this aim is achieved in a state of mutual arousal, and the interpersonal character of arousal determines the nature of the 'union' that is sought. All desire is compromising, and the choice to express it or to yield to it is an *existential* choice, in which the self is, or may be, in danger. Not surprisingly, therefore, the sexual act is surrounded by prohibitions; it brings with it a weight of shame, guilt and jealousy, as well as the heights of joy and happiness. It is inconceivable that a morality of pure permission should issue from the right conception of such a compromising force, and, as I argue in *Sexual Desire*, the traditional morality, in which monogamous heterosexual union, enshrined in a vow rather than a contract, is the norm, shows far more sensitivity to what is at stake than any of the known alternatives.

If it is so difficult now to see the point of that morality, it is in part because human sexual conduct has been redescribed by the pseudo-science of sexology, and as a result not only robbed of its interpersonal intentionality, but also profoundly demoralized. In redescribing the human world in this way, we also change it. We introduce new forms of sexual feeling – shaped by the desire for an all-comprehending permission. The sexual sacrament gives way to a sexual market; and the result is a fetishism of the sexual commodity. Richard Posner, for example, in his worthless but influential book entitled *Sex and Reason* (but which should have been called *Sex and Instrumental Reason*), opens his first chapter with the following sentence: 'There is sexual behaviour, having to do mainly with excitation of the sexual organs.' In reality, of course, sexual behaviour has to do with courtship, desire, love, jealousy, marriage, grief, joy and intrigue. Such excitement as occurs is excitement of the whole person. As for the sexual organs, they can be as 'excited' (if that is the word) by a bus journey as by the object of desire. Nevertheless, Posner's description of desire is necessary, if he is to fulfil his aim of deriving a morality of sexual conduct from the analysis of cost and benefit (which, apparently, is what is meant by 'reason'). So what are the 'costs' of sexual gratification?

One is the cost of search. It is zero for masturbation, considered as a solitary activity, which is why it is the cheapest of practices. (The qualification is important: 'mutual masturbation', heterosexual or homosexual, is a form of nonvaginal intercourse, and its search costs are positive.)

Posner proceeds to consider hypothetical cases: for example, the case where a man sets a 'value' of 'twenty' on 'sex' with a 'woman of average attractiveness', and a 'value' of 'two' on 'sex' with a 'male substitute'. If you adopt such language, then you have made woman (and man too) into a sex object and sex into a commodity. You have redescribed the human world as a world of things; you have abolished the sacred, the prohibited and the protected, and presented sex as a relation between aliens: 'Th'expence of spirit in a waste of shame', in Shakespeare's famous words. Posner's language is opaque to *what is wanted* in sexual desire; it reduces the other person to an instrument of pleasure, a means of obtaining something that could have been provided equally by another person, by an animal, by a rubber doll or a piece of Kleenex.

Well, you might say, why not, if people are happier that way? In whose interest is it, to retain the old form of desire, with its individualizing intentionality, its hopeless yearnings, its furies and jealousies, its lifelong commitments and lifelong griefs?

Modern philosophers shy away from such questions, although they were much discussed in the ancient world. Rather than consider the long-term happiness and fulfilment of the individual, the modern philosopher tends to reduce the problem of sexual morality to one of rights – do we have a right to engage in, or to forbid, this or that sexual practice? From such a question liberal conclusions follow as a matter of course; but it is a question that leaves the ground of sexual morality unexplored. This ground is not to be discovered in the calculus of rights and duties, but in the theory of virtue. What matters in sexual morality is the distinction between virtuous and vicious dispositions. I have already touched on this distinction in the last chapter, when considering the basis of our moral thinking. I there emphasized the role of virtue in creating the foundations of moral order. But it is also necessary, if we are to give objective grounds for the pursuit of virtue, to show how the happiness and fulfilment of the person are furthered by virtue and jeopardized by vice. This, roughly speaking, is the task that Aristotle set himself in the *Nicomachean Ethics*, in which he tried to show that the deep questions of morality concern the education of the moral being, rather than the rules governing his adult conduct. Virtue belongs to character, rather than to the rules of social dialogue, and arises through an extended process of moral development. The virtuous person is disposed to choose those courses of action which contribute to his flourishing – his flourishing, not just as an animal, but as a rational being or person, as that which he essentially is. In educating a child I am educating his habits, and it is therefore clear that I shall always have a reason to inculcate virtuous habits, not only for my sake, but also for his own.

At the same time, we should not think of virtue as a *means* only. The virtuous person is the one who has the right choice of *ends*. Virtue is the disposition to want, and therefore to choose, certain things for their own sakes, despite the warring tendency of appetite. Courage, for example, is the disposition to choose the honourable course of action, in face of danger. It is the disposition to *overcome fear*, for the sake of that judged to be right. All rational beings have an interest in acquiring courage, since without it they can achieve what they *really* want only by luck, and only in the absence of adversity. Sexual virtue is similar: the disposition to choose the course of action judged to be right, despite temptation. Education should be directed towards the special kind of temperance which shows itself, sometimes as chastity, sometimes as fidelity, sometimes as passionate desire, according to the 'right judgement' of the subject. The virtuous person desires the person whom he may also love, who can and will return his desire, and to whom he may commit himself. In the consummation of such a desire there is neither shame nor humiliation, and the 'nuptuality' of the erotic impulse finds the space that it needs in order to flourish.

The most important feature of traditional sexual education is summarized in anthropological language as the 'ethic of pollution and taboo'. The child was taught to regard his body as sacred, and as subject to pollution by misperception or misuse. The sense of pollution is by no means a trivial side-effect of the 'bad sexual encounter': it may involve a penetrating disgust, at oneself, one's body, one's situation, such as is experienced by the victim of rape. Those sentiments express the tension contained within our experience of embodiment. At any moment we can become 'mere body', the self driven from its incarnation, and its habitation ransacked. The most important root idea of sexual morality is that I am in my body, not as a 'ghost in the machine', but as an incarnate self. My body is identical with me: subject and object are merely two aspects of a single thing, and sexual purity is the guarantee of this. Sexual virtue does not forbid desire: it simply ensures the status of desire as an interpersonal feeling. The child who learns 'dirty habits' detaches his sex from himself, sets it outside himself as something curious and alien in the world of objects. His fascinated enslavement to the body is also a withering of desire, a scattering of erotic energy and a loss of union with the other. Sexual virtue sustains the *subject* of desire, making him present as a self in the very act which overcomes him.

Traditional sexual education also involved a sustained war against fantasy. Fantasy plays an important part in our sexual doings, and even the most passionate and faithful lover may, in the act of love, rehearse to himself other scenes of sexual abandon than the one in which he is engaged. Nevertheless, there is truth in the Freudian contrast between fantasy and reality, and in the belief that the first is in some way destructive of the second. Fantasy replaces the real, resistant, objective world with a pliant substitute – and that, indeed, is its purpose. Life in the actual world is difficult and embarrassing. Most of all it is difficult and embarrassing in our confrontation with other people who, by their very existence as subjects, rearrange things in defiance of our will. It requires a great force, such as the force of sexual desire, to overcome the self-protection that shields us from intimate encounters. It is tempting to take refuge in substitutes, which neither embarrass us nor resist the impulse of our spontaneous cravings. The habit grows of creating a compliant world of desire, in which unreal objects become the focus of real emotions, and the emotions themselves are rendered incompetent to participate in the building of personal relations. The fantasy blocks the passage to reality, which becomes inaccessible to the will. In this process the fantasy Other, since he is entirely the instrument of my will, becomes an object for me, one among many substitutes defined purely in terms of a sexual use. The sexual world of the fantasist is a world without subjects, in which others appear as objects only. And should the fantasy take possession of him so far as to require that another person submit to it, the result is invariably indecent, tending to rape. The words that I quoted from Richard Posner are indecent in just the way that one must expect, when people no longer see the object of desire as a subject, wanted as such.

Sexual morality returns us, then, to the great conundrum

around which these chapters have revolved: the conundrum of the subject, and his relation to the world of space and time. Can we go further along the road to the unsayable? And if so, by what means of transport?

11

Music

Rilke hints at an answer to our question. 'Being,' he wrote in *Sonnets to Orpheus*, 'is still enchanted for us':

> Words still go softly out towards the unsayable.
> And music, always new, from palpitating stones
> Builds in useless space its godly home.

What exactly *is* music, and why do we locate it in a space – however useless – of its own?

Music is, or resides in, sound. But that is not a helpful thing to say, if we do not know what sound is. It is tempting to divide the world into things (tables, chairs, animals, people) and their properties. But sounds don't fit into either category. Sounds are not properties of the objects that emit them: they do not *inhere* in objects, as colours, shapes and sizes do. But nor are they things. Sounds, unlike things, *occur*; they do not fill physical space in the way that things do, nor do they have boundaries. A sound occurs only if it is produced in some way, and it ceases when the mode of production ceases. In a nutshell, sounds are not things or properties, but events, standing in relations of cause and effect to other events.

However, they are events of a peculiar kind. In most other cases we identify events by observing the changes in things. A car crash is an event, in which a car changes in respect of its properties and position. We understand the event, by understanding the change. In the case of sound, however, nothing changes. The sound occurs – but it is not a property of anything. It is self-sufficient, and we may hear it while having no knowledge of its cause. It is, so to speak, an event in which no *thing* participates – a 'pure event'. This is a very odd kind of entity, for a variety of reasons. Suppose you observe a car crash, and I ask you, 'How many events are you witnessing?' You would probably be stuck for a reply. The crash is one event, if you mean to refer merely to the change in the car: but there is much more that happens – to the people inside, to the road, to the wheels of the car, the headlights; you could go on forever. There are as many events as there are changes in things. But you don't have to count them. Events do not exist *over and above* the changes in things, and the only items in the world that you need to identify in order to refer to events are the things in which they occur.

In the case of sounds, however, we have no such easy way of answering the question 'How many?' When a violin and a flute sound in unison, it is arbitrary whether we say there is one sound or two: we have only the vaguest concept of the 'individual' sound, and seem to get by without settling questions of identity and difference. But sounds are objective: they are part of reality, and not to be confused with the auditory experiences through which we perceive them. Imagine that you enter a room and hear the first bars of Beethoven's Fifth Symphony. You leave the room and return a minute later to hear the start of the development section. Would it not be natural to conclude that the symphony had been sounding in your absence – that the sounds of the work had persisted unheard in the room where first you encountered them? In other words, is it not natural to distinguish the sound – which really exists out there – from the experience of hearing it, which exists only in me?

Not all sounds are music. There are noises, shouts, words and murmurings which, while they may occur in music, are not in themselves music. When does sound become music? Pitch is not the decisive factor: there are pitched sounds which are not music (sirens, peals of bells, tonic languages), and music which involves no pitched sounds (African drum music, for example). Nor is rhythm the decisive factor, if you mean by rhythm the regularity of a sound-pattern: for this is a feature of all normal machines. Nor is harmony decisive: whenever I switch on this computer it emits an A minor chord, with added seventh and ninth, which is about as far from music as anything that occurs in my study.

The question is best approached by asking another: what is it to *hear* a sound as music? Sounds heard as music are heard in a special kind of relation to one another. They appear within a musical 'field of force'. The transformation is comparable to that which occurs when we hear a sound as a word. The word 'bang' consists of a sound. This sound could occur in nature, yet not have the character of a word. What makes it the word that it is, is the grammar of a language, which mobilizes the sound and transforms it into a word with a specified role: it designates a sound or an action in English, an emotion in German. When hearing this sound as a word, I hear the 'field of force' supplied by grammar. Likewise, to hear a sound as music is not merely to hear it, but also to *order* it, in a certain kind of relation to other actual and possible sounds. A sound, ordered in this way, becomes a 'tone'.

When we hear tones we hear their musical implications in something like the way we hear the grammatical implications of words in a language. Of course, we probably don't know the theory of musical organization, and cannot say in words what is going on when the notes of a Haydn quartet sound so right and logical. We have only *tacit* knowledge of the musical grammar (if grammar is the word for it), just as we have a tacit knowledge of the grammar of English. Our knowledge of the principles of musical organization is expressed not in theories but in acts of recognition.

Tones in music are heard in a space of their own. They do not mingle with the sounds of the world around them, although they may be drowned by them. Music exists in its own world, and is lifted free from the world of objects. Nor do we hear tones in music as belonging to the causal order. The middle C that we hear does not strike us as the effect of someone blowing on a clarinet; rather it is a response to the B that preceded it, and calls in turn for the E that follows. When Brahms hands the second theme of the last movement of the B-flat piano concerto from orchestra to piano and back again, we hear a single melody jump electrically across these poles. Each note follows in sequence as though indifferent to the world of physical causes, and as though responding only to its predecessor and to the force that it inherits from the musical line. There is a 'virtual causality' that generates tone from tone in the musical line, even when the tones themselves are produced by quite different physical means. The physical world here sinks away into the background.

The virtual causality of the melodic line operates in a virtual space. The pitch spectrum for us has a 'high' and a 'low'. Music rises and falls in a one-dimensional space, and we have a clear impression both of the rapidity of the music, and of the distance through which it passes. Pitches define locations, and intervals measure distances. Chords can be filled, hollow, stretched, packed, or dense: and these spatial descriptions capture what we hear, when we hear the chords as music.

As soon as you examine the matter with a philosophical eye, however, you will see that those spatial descriptions are deeply mysterious. Suppose a melody begins with the clarinet playing middle C, and moves upward to E on the trumpet. You hear a movement through musical space, and also a change of timbre. But what exactly moves? Obviously C does not move to E, since C is always and essentially the pitch which it is. Nor does the clarinet 'move' to the trumpet. Besides, in the musical experience, 'clarinet' is the description of a colour, not a cause. The more you look at it, the harder it is to find anything in the musical space that actually *moves*: the melody itself does not move, being a sequence of discrete pitches, each of which is fixed forever at the 'place' where it is heard. The 'useless space' of Rilke's sonnet is indeed useless, for it is not a space at all, but only the appearance of a space.

Nevertheless, we hear it as a space, and the experience of movement is ineliminable. Moreover it is a space which is very like a one-dimensional physical space in other ways. We have already seen that there is a virtual causality which operates between events in this space: the tones of a melody are responses to the tones which precede them, and causes of the tones to come. It is also a space through which forces exert themselves: gravitational and magnetic forces, which bend tones in different directions and with different strengths. When music cadences from a dominant seventh onto the tonic, with the seventh leading, the dominant in the bass pulls the seventh down onto the third of the tonic. At the beginning of the *Rite of Spring*, after the bassoon has played in A minor for a bar, the horn enters on C-sharp, and you hear the melody push this C-sharp away from it and out of the musical line. The bassoon has established a field of force, which is exerting itself against the intruder. Tones become lighter and easier to carry as they rise, while those in the bass are heavy and, when filled with close harmony, painful to lift – so that cellos, bassoons and basses, at the end of Tchaikovsky's Sixth Symphony, collapse under the burden, and the music breaks and dies. Melodies sink and soar, they push against barriers and enter into places of rest and repose. Music is activity and gesture, and as we listen we move along with it, with no consciousness that the forces and fields against which we exert ourselves are not present in the music too.

How is this 'useless space' organized? It is normal to suggest that the crucial components in musical organization, apart from pitch, are three: rhythm, melody and harmony. But how are these defined? When you hear a rhythm, what exactly do you hear? If sounds occur in a regular sequence, you may hear them as organised rhythmically – but you may equally not do so (as when overhearing the clicking of the wheels of a railway carriage). And sounds arranged irregularly might be immensely rhythmical, like the last movement of the *Rite of Spring*. It seems that, when we hear a rhythm, we group the sounds into measures, and again into beats within each measure, in such a way as to allow stresses and accents to ride on the surface of a wave. This wave is not there, in the sounds – for they could be grouped in countless contrasting ways. But it is there in the way that we hear the sounds, imbuing them in our perception with a force that ties them together, and induces a constantly fluctuating force.

What now of melody? This phenomenon too, which seems so easy to recognize, is immensely hard to pin down. When we hear a melody we hear something begin, at a definite point in time. But what begins? And where exactly? A melody introduced by an upbeat, like the main theme of the last movement of Brahms' First Symphony, can be heard as beginning either on the upbeat, or on the downbeat to which it leads. For many people it begins somewhere between those two, in mid-air, so to speak. Once begun a melody proceeds through musical space – but not necessarily to a definite ending (think of the melody that opens Rachmaninov's Second Piano Concerto). Nor, while it lasts, does the melody require there to be *sound*. The main theme of the last movement of Beethoven's *Eroica* symphony consists largely of silences: but the melody continues uninterrupted through these silences, quite indifferent to the presence or absence of orchestral sound. It is almost as though the sounds *point* to the melody, which exists elsewhere, in a 'useless space' of its own. Here is a striking illustration of the distinction between the physical world of sounds, and the 'intentional' world of music.

The difficulties that we have in defining melody are duplicated in the case of harmony. Both melodies and chords are 'unities': musical entities with distinct parts, which are nevertheless heard as *one*. Yet they are unities of different kinds: the one a unity across time, the other a unity of simultaneous tones. Not every sequence is a melody, and not every 'simultaneity' a chord. Both diachronous and synchronous unity in music admit of many varieties. Thus we distinguish, among diachronous unities, between melodies, phrases, motifs and themes. A phrase is heard as incomplete, while a motif is heard as a living, moving 'building block' – a 'palpitating stone'. Themes may be melodic or merely 'architectonic', like the theme built from fifths that opens Berg's Violin Concerto, and which could hardly be described as a melody (a 'tune').

Likewise chords exist in many varieties: consonant and dissonant, open and closed, saturated and unsaturated. Some 'demand resolution', while others stand complete in themselves. What makes a chord the chord that it is depends not merely on the tones and the intervals that compose it, but also on the musical context in which it occurs. What in Mozart would be described as a 'half diminished seventh', appears in Wagner as the famous 'Tristan chord' – the difference being not in the pitched sounds from which it is composed, but in the musical syntax which subsumes it. Tones may sound together, without forming a chord, even if they are, from the acoustic point of view, part of a single harmony. In classical counterpoint we seldom hear the simultaneities as chords, since each voice is, so to speak, running through them without pause. The unity of a chord seems to be *sui generis*: it is a unity that we 'hear in' the tones, but which is not reducible to their physical concurrence.

The critical feature of melodies, motifs and phrases is the presence of one or more 'boundaries': events which constitute a beginning and end, and which may be more or less permeable, more or less resistant to outside invasion, more or less definitive in bringing the musical movement to a close. Phrases may be open at both ends, like the three-note phrase that opens Mozart's 40th Symphony. (And here is an interesting question: when exactly does the melody 'take off': when does the upbeat end and the downbeat begin?) Or they may be closed at the beginning (i.e. not heard as a continuation of the phrase before), like the opening motif of Beethoven's Fifth Symphony; or closed at the end, like the descending scale motif in the last movement of Ravel's Concerto for the Left Hand. This phenomenon of 'closure' is often singled out by musicologists as the root of musical structure in the Western classical tradition; but the attempt to explain it in other terms invariably runs into the ground, when it is discovered that we cannot describe it, except by using metaphors borrowed from contexts which are profoundly different from the context of music.

However difficult it may be to *describe* what we hear in music, however, there is no doubt that we hear it, that it is utterly immediate and intelligible to us, and of consuming interest. In the useless space of music we hear those musical unities – the palpitating stones of melody and harmony – built into living temples in which we wander freely, released from earthly constraints. The individuals in this musical space – harmonies and melodies – are not like individuals in physical space. For one thing, they can occur simultaneously at two different places, as when one and the same melody sounds in canon. Melodies are events, whose inner structure is one of movement, but in which nothing literally moves. Harmonies too are events, whose inner structure is one of force and tension, creating valencies to which other harmonies congregate and cohere.

Music, so conceived, is not just a pleasant sound. It is the intentional object of a musical perception: that which we hear *in* sounds, when we hear them as music. The musical perception involves an imaginative grouping of tones into phrases, measures and chords; and this grouping is subject to emendation as we listen to and study what we hear. Hence music may be both understood and misunderstood: to understand is to hear an order that 'makes sense of' the sounds. By drawing someone's attention to features that he has not heard, or has not attended to, I can make the music 'click into place' for him, and the order that was previously inaudible now becomes heard. This order is not part of the world of sounds: only rational beings can perceive it, since its origin is in the self-conscious mind. When I hear music with proper understanding, I am in some sense putting myself *into* it, imbuing it with a life that originates in me. At the same time this life, projected outwards from its human prison, takes on another character: it moves freely in a useless space of its own, where bodily objects can no longer encumber it. Music therefore offers an image of the subject, released from the world of objects, and moving in response to its own caprice. It does not describe the transcendental subject: but it *shows* it, as it would be, if it *could* be shown.

The space of music is incommensurate with physical space; the time of music is likewise incommensurate with physical time. One and the same melody can be played fast or slow; the 'pure events' of music can be reversed, as when a theme is played in retrograde, or a passage runs backwards to its starting point (like the film music in Berg's *Lulu*); a motif can be played now as a melody, now as a chord

– like the Curse motif in Wagner's *Ring*. Although music cannot break free of the prison of time, the temporal order that it reveals stands in no clear relation to the order of physical time. A vast ocean of musical time lies between the great drum strokes of Mahler's Tenth Symphony: but only a few seconds separate the physical sounds; time moves slowly and sluggishly in the opening measures of Haydn's *Creation*, but rapidly, tightly and with the greatest alertness in the last movement of Mozart's *Jupiter* Symphony; time is fragmented in Webern's *Konzert* op. 24, and scattered like stars. In these and countless other ways, we find it impossible to hear music simply as a series of events in physical time, related by before and after to the events in the surrounding physical world. Each work of music occurs in its own time, built from those 'palpitating stones' that can be shifted freely in both directions. Hence we have the experience, in music, of individuals which 'take up' the time in which they occur, and exclude other individuals from being there: as the final tonic chord of a classical symphony drives all rival tones from the place it occupies. In all these respects musical time resembles space: it is a 'spatialized' representation of temporal order.

Of course, not every work of music provides these strange experiences in equal measure. It is only the greatest labour of style and architecture that can place the freely moving subject in this useless space and build there its 'godly home'. The masterpieces of music may, however, lift us from our time and space into an ideal time and space, ordered by an ideal causality, which is the causality of freedom. From the ideal time of music it is, so to speak, a small step to eternity. Sometimes, listening to a Bach fugue, a late quartet of Beethoven, or one of those infinitely spacious themes of Bruckner, I have the thought that this very movement which I hear might have been made known to me in a single instant: that all of this is only accidentally spread out in time

before me, and that it might have been made known to me
in another way, as mathematics is made known to me. For
the musical entity – be it melody or harmony – is only a
visitor to *our* time; its individuality is already emancipated
from real time, and remains undamaged by all those trans-
formations of musical time to which I referred. We may
therefore come to think of this very individual as emancipated from time entirely, and yet *remaining an individual*.
In the experience of music, therefore, we can obtain a
glimpse of what it might be, for one and the same individual,
to exist in time and in eternity. And this encounter with the
'point of intersection of the timeless with time' is also an
encounter with the pure subject, released from the world of
objects, and moving in obedience to the laws of freedom
alone.

Of course, this does not enable us to conceive how you or
I might exist in eternity. But is the difficulty of conceiving
this a final proof of its impossibility? Consider another case:
we cannot, in the nature of things, conceive of a space that
is three-dimensional, finite and yet unbounded. But we *can*
conceive of the equivalent in two-dimensional space (for
example, the surface of a sphere). Asking someone to conceive a concrete individual (a person) existing eternally
might be a little similar. We might say: You know what it is
for a melody, which exists in ideal time, to exist also in
eternity. Now suppose the same of a concrete object, in *real*,
physical time. In some such way we say: You know what it
is for a two-dimensional space to be finite but unbounded.
Now suppose the same thing in three dimensions. And of
course you cannot *imagine* it!

I don't for the moment suppose that those last thoughts
contain an answer to the problems that have be-devilled us:
those of the relation between the timeless and time, and of
the relation between subject and object. But they have taken
us some way along the route towards the unsayable, and

provided us with a guide for the last part of the journey – this guide being not philosophy but music. The philosopher should now take Wittgenstein's advice, and consign that whereof he cannot speak to silence. He should retrace his steps towards the realm of time and objects – the realm from which all our thinking arises, and to which all our thinking tends.

12

History

Self-conscious beings exist in time and are also conscious of time, as the condition to which they are bound. Unlike animals, who exist in the moment alone, they take the before and after into constant consideration. And not only the before and after of *themselves*, but the before and after of the community which contains them, and of the human race as a whole. This is especially true of modern people, who live in the light of history, and who experience the present in relation to the past. History has become a major datum of modern consciousness, and one of the phenomena that we regard ourselves as most urgently required to understand.

'Philosophy of history' means two different things. On the one hand there is the subject more or less invented by Hegel: the philosophical examination of human history, in order to discover its meaning, and the place of self-consciousness within it. On the other hand there is the attempt to explain what historical *understanding* is or ought to be, and how it relates to understanding of other kinds – such as scientific, anthropological or cultural understanding. You could express the distinction as that between the philosophy of *history*, and the philosophy of *historiography*. Both are large and controversial areas; but it would be unwise to leave the subject without a glance at them.

Hegel believed that the elucidation of history is one of the central tasks of philosophy. This is for two reasons: first, because all human institutions and collective endeavours are forms of *consciousness*, ways in which the subject is *realized* in the objective world. Secondly, because consciousness, in Hegel's view, has an evolutionary character, driven by reason to advance from more 'abstract' and 'immediate' forms to concrete and objective realities. It is possible to discover *a priori* laws of historical development, simply by reflecting on the 'dialectical' movement that is intrinsic to 'spirit' in its objective form. The philosophy of history expounds these laws, and then shows how to interpret historical events in the light of them, filtering out what is accidental, secondary or merely spectacular, and discovering the *Zeitgeist*, the 'spirit of the time', which is the inner essence of all that happens in an epoque.

This exhilarating theory had such an impact on nineteenth-century thought that even those like Marx who denounced it acquired the vision and the emotions which it inspired in its followers. Hegel's *Lectures on the Philosophy of History* remains one of the great documents of nineteenth-century culture, and one whose influence is everywhere apparent in our modern – or postmodern – world. It is apparent too in that last hesitation of mine, since it is only a kind of Hegelianism that leads us to think that the 'modern' world is over and done with, and that a new and necessary *Zeitgeist* waits in the wings. In this chapter I shall examine some of the thoughts that have led to this strange conclusion.

It is impossible to accept Hegel's philosophy of history: only gross selection, distortion and dramatization can make history look as though it were driven by the human spirit, and only the idealist metaphysics of Fichte and Hegel can make the *Zeitgeist* idea remotely plausible. Nevertheless, there is sense in the Hegelian picture – not as a philosophy of history, but as a philosophy of historiography. The study of history could not possibly offer theories that *explain* the past in the way that physics explains the rainbow. Not only are the facts too complicated; the historian has no experimental method with which to test his hypotheses and must rely on unverifiable, and as a rule unfalsifiable, conjecture. Such 'laws' as he proposes will be vast, vague and *a priori*. In the wake of Hegel attempts were made to offer a natural 'science' of history, the most famous being that of Marx, who wished to 'set Hegel on his feet', by showing that the 'laws of motion' of human society are not spiritual but 'material'. Society is driven by man's material needs, and the economic steps taken to meet them. No piece of pseudo-science has been more influential than this one, and it is a measure of its *a priori* character that every practical application of Marxist theory has led not merely to tyranny, but to social and economic collapse.

We could give up the futile project of a science of historical events, without renouncing the attempt to *understand* them. As I argued in the first chapter, there are several kinds of 'why?'-question, and only one of these is looking for a cause. When studying human action we seek for reasons. There are reasons which explain, and reasons which justify. There are also reasons which 'make an action intelligible', by enabling us to perceive it in another way. Such reasons may neither explain nor justify but simply *redescribe* the action, so as to set it in the context of our own decision-making. For example, an action changes character in my eyes, when I see it as part of a ceremony – even when I have no idea what the ceremony is for, or what part this action plays in it. I read the gestures, expressions and movements differently, and what seemed grotesque a moment ago now makes sense. Similarly a costume is perceived differently, according to whether you think of it as daily dress, as dress for a special occasion, as fancy dress, or as a uniform. In answer to the question 'Why is he wearing that costume?', you might reply, 'It is a uniform,' without saying anything definite about the intentions of the person whose costume it is. For many Parisian intellectuals it came as a *discovery* to learn that the Maoist costumes which they affected during the 1960s were a uniform. Nevertheless, seeing those costumes as a uniform, you had a greater understanding of the people who wore them. You had found the concept with which to *situate* their behaviour in the human world.

Inspired by Kant's moral theory, the romantic theologian Friedrich Schleiermacher (1768-1834) argued that the interpretation of human actions can never be accomplished by the methods employed in the natural sciences. The human act must be understood as the act of a free subject, motivated by reason, and understood through dialogue. The same is true of texts, which can be interpreted, thought Schleiermacher, only through an imaginative dialogue with their author. 'Hermeneutics' – the art of interpretation – involves the search for reasons, and the attempt to understand a text as an expression of rational activity, the very activity that is manifest in me.

A later Kantian philosopher, Wilhelm Dilthey (1833-1911), extended Schleiermacher's hermeneutical 'method' to the entire human world. We seek to understand human actions, he argued, not by explaining them in terms of external causes, but 'from within', by an act of rational self-projection that Dilthey called *Verstehen*. In understanding human life and action, we must find the concepts through which the other person perceives and acts upon the world. For example, I understand your fear of speaking in a certain place, once I conceptualize it as you do, as somewhere 'sacred'.

According to Dilthey, our ways of conceptualizing the world in everyday life do not follow the direction laid down by scientific explanation. Rather, they represent the world as 'ready for action'. I see the world under the aspect of my own freedom, and describe and respond to it accordingly. This before me is not a member of the species *Homo sapiens* but a *person*, who looks at me and smiles; that beside her is not a piece of bent organic tissue but a *chair* on which I may sit; this on the wall is not a collection of tinted chemicals but a *picture*, in which the face of a *saint* appears; and so on. In short, we do not merely enter into dialogue with each other; we are in constant dialogue with the world of objects, moulding it through our descriptions so as to align it with our rational purposes. Our categories do not *explain* the world, so much as endow it with *meaning*. When I see the Parisian intellectual's costume as a uniform, I have found its meaning, as an object of human intention and desire.

Something like that must surely be true, if the argument of previous chapters has any cogency. The stance of the subject to other subjects is interrogatory; and this interrogatory attitude spreads over objects too, conceptualizing them not as they are, but as they appear in the light of our human interests. In the case of objects, on which we can perform experiments, and which are open to our uses in every way, the concepts of our ordinary intentional understanding soon give way to other and deeper classifications, founded in scientific method. In the case of other subjects, this transition can occur only with difficulty, and only at the risk of losing sight of the matter that we are trying to understand. The 'human sciences' are really attempts to reorder the *appearance* of the human world, not so as to explore its underlying causes, but so as to enter into dialogue with it, and discover its meaning as an object of human interest.

The term 'human sciences' is the best translation we have of the German *Geisteswissenschaften*; but just as 'human' is a very bad equivalent to *Geist*, which means spirit, so is 'science' a poor equivalent for *Wissenschaft*, which also means knowledge, expertise and wisdom, as did *scientia* in Latin. These semantic points are not quibbles, since they go to the heart of Dilthey's project. The attempt to make the humanities into sciences risks the very real understanding which they contain. It sacrifices the human appearance to the non-human reality, and presents as a system of objects that which we relate to as a community of subjects.

Here, then, is the clue to the study of history. Historical categories and classifications order the past in terms of its *meaning*, as an object of rational dialogue. A valid historical category helps us to understand the 'why?' of a past action, of a past way of thinking, or of a past sequence of events, so as to see how human subjects might have acted or thought in that way. For example, the concept of the Renaissance classifies together a collection of ambitions, projects and artefacts, in terms of a common stance towards the world. By grouping the writings of Alberti, the buildings of Bramante, the political projects of the Medici and the new polyphony as 'Renaissance', we seem to increase our understanding of all of them: we are better able to interrogate them, to ask 'Why?', and to find a reason which makes sense to us. If we think of them in this way, we begin to look for parallels, to find the ways in which Brunelleschi was doing 'the same kind of thing' as Josquin, or Cosimo Medici the 'same kind of thing' as Piero della Francesca. It is not absurd to think of this kind of explanation in the terms suggested by Hegel: we are looking for the common 'spirit' of an epoch, in the hope that one action will make sense in the light of another, just as one gesture in a ceremony begins to make sense, when related to the other gestures by which it is surrounded, even though each is unintelligible alone.

There are dangers in this, of course. We might begin to mix hermeneutics with a kind of *a priori* determinism, believing that contemporaneous actions *must* express the same spirit, that, existing in Renaissance Italy, you simply *had* to be a humanist, a classicist, a believer in antiquity, a lover of pagan mythology and of polyphony built in thirds.

Hegel encourages this kind of determinism, as do the academic subjects which sprang up in the wake of his ideas – notably the history of art, which did so much to create the currently accepted periodization of our culture. Such determinism is precisely what the hermeneutical approach should avoid. A hermeneutics of history aims to understand historical events as the *free* actions of individual subjects, which nevertheless, conceived as a whole, have a common appearance or *Gestalt*. If we say that this or that event in the pattern *must* be as it is, or that, in the context of the *Gestalt*, it is *inevitable*, we are not really speaking in causal terms. The concept of inevitability that we are using is that which occurs also in aesthetic judgement: as when I say that this chord is inevitable, or that the character of Caliban is required by the play. The necessity here is a *felt* necessity, deriving from our sense of artistic form. Such artistic necessity is the highest kind of freedom, and in no way determined by the context.

The most damaging form of historical determinism arises when we try to understand present times. Historical categories, provided that they deal with times sufficiently remote, and people sufficiently mysterious, can bring us into dialogue with the matters they describe, and so advance our understanding. We see past periods and movements in dramatic terms, singling out the leading motives, the shared conceptions, and the principal points of conflict, in order to elicit the kind of order that we understand from the unity of human character. A period is like a collective person, speaking to us down the ages, in a way which permits a coherent response. This is how we should understand the Renaissance, the Middle Ages, the Reformation, the Counter-Reformation, and the Enlightenment. These periods or movements do not have clear temporal boundaries, and the aspect they present to us is often ambiguous, like the aspect of a painting. Yet we can understand them as we understand persons in a drama: they embody a pattern of human motivation, in terms of which to grasp the how and why of emotions, beliefs and desires.

When we try to see our own epoch or society in such terms, however, we at once fall out of relation with it. Historical categories are designed to apply to the *past*: they reassemble the fragments of recorded time as a coherent drama, in order that we can profitably relate to it. But this is reasonable only because we have no *other* way of relating to it, no way of interrogating the past directly, no way of changing it according to our own conceptions and ideals. We are forced to look upon it from an impassable distance, as we look upon the characters in a play. If we take the same approach to our own time, then we remove ourselves from a true engagement with it; we depersonalize the world in which we live, precisely by seeing it as a collective person. And dire results may follow from this, as they followed from Lenin's reading of Marx, and Goebbels' reading of Spengler. An aesthetic of history becomes a science of the present, and a prophecy of future things.

It is in the light of this that we should understand the fashionable concept of postmodernity. I am reluctant to add to the many definitions of 'modernity', still less to encourage the belief that the 'modern' world is all of a piece. Nevertheless, a change came into the world when people began to define themselves as modern – as in some way 'apart from' their predecessors, standing to them in some new and self-conscious relationship. And this could serve as a definition of modernity: as the condition in which people provide definitions of modernity. For there is a great difference between living in history – which, for self-conscious beings, is unavoidable – and living according to an *idea* of history, and of one's own place within it.

You might put the point in another, and more provocative way. Modern people do not live in the present. They live the pastness of the present – confronting each moment as it *will* be from the vantage-point of future time. Modern people live as though they stepped into the present from the future; and even as they seize the present moment, it is misted over by its pastness, and falls from their hands into the boundless sea of remembrance and forgetting. When people argue that the modern world is finished, that we are now entering the postmodern period of our culture, they are in a sense expressing their adherence to modernity in its latest form, inventing another historical category through which to summarize and pre-empt the past of the present moment, and to look on the world as a perpetually disappearing thing. But they are also expressing their sense that this very practice, of seeing oneself as 'one step further on', has lost its former appeal.

Looked at from the point of view of intellectual history, the 'modern' world arose from the scientific revolution of the seventeenth century, from the ideal of secular and democratic government, from the industrial revolution, and from the pressure of education and emancipation which led to the collapse of old ideas of sovereignty, and to the belief that the individual could never be bound by an obligation which had not been chosen by himself. Those great events belong together, as cause or effect of the rise of science; and the term 'Enlightenment' is now frequently used to refer to them, having been introduced by Kant in one of the first of many attempts to write 'the history of the present moment'. Together they exalt the idea of 'progress' into a ruling principle in every sphere of human endeavour, whether scientific, cultural or political. And it may very well be that this idea has lost its sovereign place in our thinking – and with good reason, when you consider the damage it has caused.

The French philosopher Jean-François Lyotard puts the point somewhat differently. In *The Postmodern Condition* (1979) he argues that modernity should be characterized in terms of certain 'narratives' (he actually calls them, for no good reason, 'metanarratives') of 'legitimation': by which he means doctrines, stories, theories and ideas which tend to the conclusion that institutions and practices are well-founded and legitimate, that all's well with the world, whether or not God is in his Heaven. Traditional societies derive their legitimacy from backward-looking narratives – the myths, archetypes and religions which embed the tribe in history. The narratives which characterize the modern era are forward-looking, pointing to a future state of emancipation and higher knowledge; present privations and injustices are rendered tolerable when they are shown to be stages on the way to that higher state, or intolerable when discovered to be obstructions. And the future state – the Idea to be realized (freedom, enlightenment, socialism, prosperity, equality, and so on) – has 'legitimating value' because it is universal. The narratives of modernity are 'cosmopolitan', to use another of Kant's expressions: they are promises made to all mankind.

The postmodern condition comes about when such narratives have ceased to be believable. The last gasp of hope has been breathed, and we stand amid the ruin of our dear illusions, looking on a world the legitimacy of which can be ceaselessly questioned, but never confirmed. The fund of affirmation has at last run dry, and nothing remains to us save the choice between despair and irony.

No such thing could possibly be true. If it *seems* true, it is because the writer has been tempted by the 'history of the present moment' into a posture of determinism. If we think that historical categories show us how things *must* be, and that the era in which we live is intelligible only as the era of postmodernity, then we may find ourselves having to choose between postmodernist irony, and postmodern despair. The correct response to the diagnosis, however, is to forget about both the modern and the postmodern condition, and look seriously at the human world. If there is no legitimacy to be found in the idea of progress, then let us renounce those forward-looking attitudes which make such use of it, and study things as they were and are. A small dose of philosophy will persuade us that people have *always* been wrong to look to the future for the test of legitimacy, rather than to the past. For the future, unlike the past, is unknown and untried. A host of respectable modern thinkers were aware of this fact and tried (against the pressure of half-educated enthusiasm) to remind their contemporaries of it: Burke, for example, Coleridge, Tocqueville, even Hegel. The modernist adulation of the future should be seen as an expression of despair, not of hope; and the postmodernist irony is merely an attempt to recapture an ingredient in all true philosophy – in all philosophy that recognizes that we are both subject and object, and that between these two lies an impassable barrier through which at every moment we must nevertheless pass.

In those last few paragraphs I have been considering a question in the history of ideas. If you take philosophy seriously, you will soon recognize that the history of philosophy is a very different subject from the history of ideas. The history of philosophy is a branch of *philosophy*. It consists in the exposition and criticism of arguments, lifted from their historical context and assessed for their validity. Ideas are studied for the light that they cast on questions that still concern us, like the questions that have occupied the discussions in this book. The history of ideas, by contrast, is a branch of *historiography*. An historian of ideas is interested in the origin and influence of an idea; but he may be indifferent to its truth or validity. A philosopher ought not to be interested in those 'narratives of legitimation' which fascinate Lyotard: for they never *were* believable, not even at the time when first they were uttered. Most people cannot think clearly or consistently; hence absurd conceptions tend to have more historical impact than serious arguments, and minor thinkers occupy the foreground in the history of ideas. The history of ideas is not a history of the believable, but of the will to believe.

If we step back from the history of ideas into the realm of pure philosophy, we find that neither the modern nor the postmodern are concepts which are helpful to us. Philosophical answers may not be eternal; but the questions recur. And that is what we must expect. Our condition, properly seen, is neither temporal nor timeless. As Nietzsche saw, self-consciousness requires 'eternal recurrence', in which everything we think and do is both now and always. The effort to say what this means is the perennial task of philosophy; and it is a task that is fulfilled only by relinquishing it – by taking the reader to the point where the music of the spheres can at last be heard, and he attains that 'condition of complete simplicity', costing, Eliot adds in parenthesis, not less than everything.

Further Reading

I have tried to give an overview of the subject in *Modern Philosophy*, London 1994. This contains a Study Guide, which takes the reader through the contemporary literature, and tries to impose some order upon it. I have also written an introduction to the history of modern philosophy: *A Short History of Modern Philosophy*, 2nd edn., London 1995. Whatever the faults of those books, they have, for me, the singular merit of presenting the subject as I think it to be. Others would not agree with my approach. Among reputable alternatives, the following are noteworthy:

Bertrand Russell, *The Problems of Philosophy*, London 1912.

A.J. Ayer, *The Central Questions of Philosophy*, London 1973.

A.C. Grayling, ed., *Philosophy: a Guide through the Subject*, Oxford 1995.

Simon Blackburn, ed., *A Dictionary of Philosophy*, Oxford 1995.

For a scrupulous, if occasionally somewhat dated, account of the history of philosophy, the reader should consult the magisterial work by Frederick Copleston, in 12 vols: *History of Philosophy*, London 1950 onwards.

Index

● MORE DUCKBACK NON-FICTION ●

Diary of a Man in Despair
Friedrich Reck-Malleczewen £6.99 Paperback 0 7156 3100 4

The fascinating journal of a Prussian aristocrat written between 1936 and 1944.

Cleopatra's Wedding Present
Travels through Syria
Robert Tewdwr Moss   £6.99 Paperback   0 7156 3099 7

Robert Tewdwr Moss describes his travel experiences with rare charm and aplomb.

The Way of Hermes
Translated by Clement Salaman, Dorine van Oyen, William D. Wharton, Jean-Pierre Mahé   £6.99 Paperback 0 7156 3093 8

The *Corpus Hermeticum* is a collection of short philosophical treatises, a powerful fusion of Greek and Egyptian thought, written in Greek in Alexandria between the first and third centuries AD.

One Woman's War
Eve-Ann Prentice   £6.99 Paperback   0 7156 3104 7

A personal account of the Balkan war, hailed by Harold Pinter as 'a powerful and important book'.

The Pig: A British History
Julian Wiseman   £6.99 Paperback   0 7156 3092 X

'Full of delightful pictures of the different breeds. Gripping'
Independent

The Captain
The Life and Times of Simon Raven
Michael Barber   £6.99 Paperback   0 7156 3138 1

Tremendously well-received biography of the late Simon Raven, one of Britain's most idiosyncratic and talented characters.

On Beauty and Being Just
Elaine Scarry   £6.99 Paperback   0 7156 3134 9

A lucid philosophical critique on the interpretation of beauty.

Horace: A Life
Peter Levi   £6.99 Paperback   0 7156 3136 5

The first comprehensive biography for 40 years of the life of the great Roman poet.

The Uncollected Dorothy Parker
Edited by Stuart Y Silverstein   £6.99 Pbk   0 7156 3135 7

122 forgotten pieces displaying the raw talent and dexterity of America's most renowned cynic.

A Short Walk Down Fleet Street
From Beaverbrook to Boycott
Alan Watkins   £6.99 Paperback   0 7156 3143 8

'entertaining and enlightening ... a series of splendid pen portraits'

Sunday Telegraph

'The Law is a Ass'
An Illustrated Anthology of Legal Quotations
Compiled & Edited by Ronald Irving £6.99 Pbk 0 7156 3142 X

An entertaining compendium of witty, cynical and profound observations, sayings and anecdotes about the law.

An Intelligent Person's Guide to Ethics
Mary Warnock   £6.99 Paperback   0 7156 3089 X

'one of the best guides to ethics available'

Ray Monk, *Sunday Telegraph*

An Intelligent Person's Guide to History
John Vincent   £6.99 Paperback   0 7156 3090 3

'not only is Vincent one of the great historians of 19th-century British politics, he is also that rarest of things in academic history: a witty prose stylist'

Niall Ferguson, *Daily Telegraph*

An Intelligent Person's Guide to Dickens
Michael Slater   £6.99 Paperback   0 7156 3088 1

'Michael Slater has an encyclopaedic knowledge of Dickens's writings'

Times Literary Supplement

An Intelligent Person's Guide to Modern Ireland
John Waters   £6.99 Paperback   0 7156 3091 1

'John Waters skilfully attacks those who decry any sense of nationalism or belittle any aspiration that the two parts of Ireland should be united'

Michael O'Toole, *Irish News* (Belfast)

Lads: Love poetry of the trenches
Edited by Martin Taylor   £6.99 Paperback   0 7156 3145 4

A remarkable anthology of many largely unknown poems from the trenches.

Poetic Gems
Introduction by Billy Connolly
William McGonagall   £6.99 Paperback   0 7156 3151 9

William McGonagall, known as the Greatest Bad Verse Writer of his age, was unrecognised during his lifetime but now has admirers all over the world.

The Handsomest Sons in the World!
Harold Carlton   £6.99 Paperback   0 7156 3158 6

An autobiographical romp through north-west London and Soho in the 50s.

Reach for the Ground: The downhill struggle of Jeffrey Bernard
Foreword by Peter O'Toole
Jeffrey Bernard   £6.99 Paperback   0 7156 3150 0

An irresistible collection of the best of Jeffrey Bernard's **Low Life** columns.

The Dream Dictionary for the Modern Dreamer
Tim Etchells   £6.99 Paperback   0 7156 3154 3

A mischievous glimpse into the contemporary subconscious and a playful, irreverent portrait of 21st century life.

'the perfect work for fragmented, poorly understood lives'
Nicholas Lezard, *Guardian*

A Memoir: People & Places
Mary Warnock   £6.99 Paperback   0 7156 3141 1

Philosopher Mary Warnock reflects on some of the people who have influenced or intrigued her throughout her career.

The Undiscovered Chekhov: Fifty-One New Stories
Translated by Peter Constantine   £6.99 Pbk   0 7156 3155 1

Peter Constantine's award-winning translation casts new light on the development of the great playwright's development.

SIEGFRIED SASSOON Volume I: The Making of a War Poet
Jean Moorcroft Wilson   £9.99 Paperback   0 7956 3121 7

The first volume of Moorcroft Wilson's critically acclaimed biography of one of the twentieth century's finest poets.

ORDER FORM (BLOCK CAPITALS PLEASE)

SURNAME _____ FIRST NAME _____

ADDRESS _____

_____

_____ POSTCODE _____

METHOD OF PAYMENT (PLEASE TICK AS APPROPRIATE)

☐ Invoice to my Grantham Book Services account
☐ By cheque (payable to Duckworth Publishers)
☐ Please send account opening details (trade customers only)
☐ By credit card (Access/ Visa / Mastercard / Amex)

Card no: ☐ ☐ ☐ ☐ ☐ ☐ ☐ ☐ ☐ ☐ ☐ ☐ ☐ ☐ ☐ ☐

Expiry date: __ / __ / __ Authorising Signature: _____

POSTAGE (Private customers) Please note that the following postage and packing charges should be added to your order:

UK deliveries: £3 on orders up to £16; £4 on orders over £16
Export surface: £3.50 for first book + £0.50 for each additional book
Export airmail: £7 for the first book + £2 for each additional book

QTY	ISBN	TITLE	PRICE	TOTAL

TOTAL £_____

To: Sales Dept, Duckworth, 61 Frith Street, London W1D 3JL
Tel:+44 (0) 20 7434 4242 Fax: +44 (0) 20 7434 4420
Heidi@duckworth-publishers.co.uk